DAVID GENTLEMAN
IN THE
COUNTRY

DAVID GENTLEMAN
IN THE COUNTRY

FULL CIRCLE EDITIONS

Contents

Introduction

This book is about the country as opposed to the city, and in particular about a place my family and I have grown to know over thirty-five years of coming and going – not as regular weekenders but as work, children and grandchildren have determined. It isn't about the county as a whole – most of the places drawn here are those on our doorstep, the others we could drive to within about half an hour. But however local its subject matter, some aspects of it are characteristic of Suffolk and some even of the countryside in general; and though they may seem ordinary and permanent enough, they are often both beautiful and vulnerable.

I first got to know East Anglia by cycling there with my father as a boy and then, after my parents had moved to the Essex/Suffolk border, by driving around the Stour valley with him. I was also attracted there by my work. My first post-student watercolours, when for a while I rented a flat on the river Stour at Manningtree, were of the maltings at Mistley and the thin strip of Suffolk on the far bank of the estuary. Some of my early lithographs were of Suffolk subjects – Saxtead windmill and Orford tide-mill, the Snape maltings, Heveningham Hall, the Abbey gatehouse at Bury St Edmunds, Mistley Quay and Orford Castle. Then in my mid-thirties I went to Helmingham in Suffolk to illustrate a book by the writer

George Ewart Evans, whose daughter Sue I later married. Thirty-five years ago, needing a place where I could paint and our young children could have a change from their life in London, we bought the end quarter of a Suffolk longhouse in an equally obscure part of the county. (We later expanded through the wall into the quarter next door.) It had a garden next to a stream, was at the edge of a small village surrounded by fields and woodland, and was near enough to the coast for the family to bathe and enjoy the beach while I drew the crumbling cliffs and the shingle shore.

The appeal of the nearby village, and indeed of the whole area, was and is its unremarkableness. Apart from the wooden angels and the very Victorian painted ceiling in the church, there's nothing much except the pub to attract visitors; the nearest teashop is five miles away. Most of the village buildings are fairly low-key. There is just one remarkable exception. A mile or so away, glimpsed beyond its own lake, is a fine Palladian mansion, surrounded by the recently restored landscaping of its parkland. On its further horizons are many acres of recently-planted saplings that will in due course become a ring of woodland.

Amid and around all this is the seemingly indestructible beauty of our immediate surroundings – the fields, the trees, the stream, the remaining or replanted hedgerows, and the often prairie-like fields between them. Now as in the past the main industry is still farming. Out of our windows we can see the changing crops – over the years wheat, oil seed rape, barley, peas, beans and cabbages – and compare their colours and textures and rates of growth. We can also hear in the background the current country sounds; for on dry August and September days and nights the whole place throbs to the sound of heavy machinery as gigantic yet stately combine harvesters gobble up several fields of rape or corn in an afternoon. The house trembles as the harvest-time stream of tractors, their trailers brimming with corn, belt past our garden gate.

Suffolk landscapes in this area are green and gently undulating, with white-painted houses gleaming against often dark and magnificent skies. Fields, woods, lanes and paths still remain part of a generously subsidized farming economy that on balance sustains rather than harms the appearance of the environment. On the horizons concrete water-towers of the thirties now bristle with IT aerials, and pylons sail across it regardless, yet on the other hand many aspects of the surrounding rural landscapes and skies – apart from the vapour-trails – look pretty much as they must have been for centuries.

In our local landscape there are also many details or remnants of the past: fine ancient oaks, a woodland walk through a tunnel of hornbeams beside the stream that passes our garden, WW2 pillboxes and the skeletal remains of a wartime Nissen hut now impenetrably overgrown. Yet even during our own time here there have been significant changes to the area at large. It has been penetrated by faster roads; there is a fast mainline railway service to London forty minutes' drive away, its station now surrounded by a vast commuter car-park. A more accessible but slower and less frequent line through enchanting countryside is only twenty minutes away from us in the nearest small town. Here, disused maltings have been turned into flats and an arts centre, an old house into a picture gallery. There is a handy new supermarket which has taken away from the high street shops much of their trade, forcing them to turn into hair-dressers, cafés, takeaways and charity shops. The town is usually busy with shoppers. But in the village and the fields for most of the year there are few people to be seen except for those whizzing anonymously past in their cars. In the village houses, the farm-workers and weekenders have largely given way to couples who have opted to leave London or its suburbs for good.

Suffolk is somewhat out on a limb, on the way to no-place in particular, reached via Liverpool Street or through the East End rather than through the smarter West End, and consequently less severely suburbanised than Surrey or the Cotswolds. Development in this part of Suffolk exists but is not yet a scourge. Its most famously beautiful villages are concentrated more in the south-west than in the north-east of the county. Hereabouts there are fewer historic small buildings than in for example Lavenham or Sudbury; the churches, though architecturally often interesting, are generally less spectacular and there is only one great house. But the natural landscape, despite its unpretentiousness, is often extremely beautiful.

The county's general flatness means that even though its modest hills are more noticeable than in Cambridgeshire or Norfolk they never get you much higher up: there are no dramatic Derbyshire or Cumbrian-type heights to provide amazing viewpoints here. In Suffolk really distant views are with one important exception rare and seldom dramatic. This exception is wherever the countryside encounters or is penetrated by the sea. My final chapters are about these estuarine and marine aspects of Suffolk that we grew to know through many expeditions with children and grandchildren.

What makes any landscape beautiful or interesting? Since the obvious things like grandeur and distant magnificence are thin on the ground in Suffolk, lesser things become important - the freshness of the air and the greenery, the dampness in fields, ponds, puddles, and in the earth itself; the textures of furrows, stubble, bark and tyre-tracks; the close details of plants and wildlife. Above all there is the landscape's down-to-earth reality. It has been around for a long time, in the permanent, unchanging lie of the land, the shapes of hills and valleys, the courses of streams and rivers: all these are timeless. And even more recent things are still centuries old – trees, fields, even hedges, are all reminders of our long-standing human presence. But of course much of what one

sees, mostly man-made, has changed more recently still, even within the last few decades: farming methods, the constantly intensifying mechanisation of even timeless activities like ploughing and reaping and ways of baling and packaging hay and straw; different kinds of tractors, combines, SUVs and Land-Rovers; the new materials and construction methods that have transformed barns from picturesque wooden relics into industrial and financial-scale structures.

Besides these practical changes there are new views, new landscapes, caused as policies towards conservation, fallow land, planning and landscaping, roads and traffic have evolved. New technologies like wind farming, recent materials like the protective plastic sheeting which from a distance seem to transform the fields they cover into lakes or inlets; new developments like the computers which can now steer tractors and combines and tell the driver and the farmer the precise quality and yield of a crop in a particular piece of a field even as it's being harvested.

Even so one can't help sensing that towns and cities are gradually but relentlessly seeping into the countryside which provides us not only with food but with space. Its fragile beauty and reality remind us of the pervasive processes of nature that we damage at our peril. It also makes city dwellers like me reconsider our assumptions. Cities provide activities, spectacle, jobs, variety and stimulus. In big cities, houses are far dearer, food a little cheaper, the weather and seasons things that can be easily ignored; light, air and noise pollution are inescapable; people and traffic are everywhere, but social options such as choosing to meet people or preferring anonymity are equally available.

In the country on the other hand, anonymity is impossible since anything you do in a village is noticed. And there are far fewer people, less interruption, fewer distractions but more concentration. Season and weather are inescapable. There's also less pollution – the nights are darker and quieter, the stars brighter, than in the city. Natural processes can be seen on every hand. It's good, and not only for children, to be reminded what the bread and vegetables and apples on the table looked like before they got there, how the pigs, sheep and hens lived before they became bacon and lamb and chicken. All these are set against the continuity of natural changes, slow or quick: the seasons changing through the year, vegetation from week to week as plants and crops grow, develop and die; the constantly altering weather and light, the hour-by-hour or even minute-by-minute contrasts of colour and tone and the unfolding dramas of mist, sunrise, presence and position of shadows, a shower falling, a cloud shadow approaching you across a field or, when it's overcast, a short burst of sunlight surprising you by spotlighting a patch of distant countryside. When you're drawing outside you can't help noticing these things.

But why, now we've all got cameras, should anyone any longer bother to draw landscape at all? Well, drawing anything makes one look and think; and drawing in the open – especially when there is warm sun, a light breeze, pleasant scents and sounds, even threatening clouds - can be a good experience: one's in nobody's way and it's fun. It also helps one to understand why things look as they do – why trees have twisted shapes, why fields and streams have come to be where they are, how a cloud in one bit of the sky can cast a shadow over another – and to wonder at the way natural forms come into being, grow, flourish, bloom, die, decay and renew themselves. Simply drawing a landscape, however well or badly you seems to be doing it, makes you realise that you're learning something, that you're looking harder at it, discovering things about it that you've never really seen. Noticing, like thinking, is worthwhile and rewarding – a significant part of one's experience, one's life.

House

Our house forms part of a Suffolk longhouse, quite hard to see from a distance though at harvest-time you can glimpse it from the field opposite through a gap in the hedge. It is set back a few yards from the road, and there are four front doors, each of which opens onto a small garden with its own wooden wicket gate. There were four household units in the terrace when we arrived, of which we bought the end one on the left; after a few years our next-door neighbour left and we bought his too. The roof is tiled, the walls white-painted plaster over wattle-and-daub.

Church Terrace is a timber-framed structure on two floors plus an attic and cellar. Its history is obscure but it was probably built between 1570 and 1590, possibly as a farmhouse or a parsonage or even both, since the parson would have had to farm the glebe land around the church. From outside, however, it doesn't look nearly as old as this: at first glance the whole terrace could be Victorian, because it was partially rebuilt as four dwellings in the mid- to late-19th century. Its doors and windows were renewed with wooden porches and hood mouldings or eyebrows above the new windows, making a strikingly uniform repeat pattern across the whole front of the building, but their slight unevenness confirms the rather more haphazard nature of the original building behind them.

The roof has the comfortable sag of an old building, and the gable and its bargeboards slope outwards. The timber-framed building stands on a brick base, painted black. When we bought the second cottage in the row with its own bits of garden, we kept the small front bit separate behind its hedge to maintain the individual identity of each unit. After we'd been there for a few years we rashly planted an oak tree cutting nearer the house than we should have. There are several apple trees, much propped up, and a crab apple, a laburnum (now dying) and a hawthorn. In the front hedge are several lilac bushes, in the flowerbeds bluebells and hollyhocks, poppies and teasels and evening primroses. It's fun watching these in the warm summer evenings when the tight spirals of the yellow buds are about to spring open, though it's difficult to be looking at just the right instant. I also enjoy dead-heading them the next morning – the peak of my gardening skills. These skills had to be reined in. There used to be a beautiful and extensive rose in the front hedge, but once when Sue was out shopping I helpfully cut it out with the secateurs, thinking it was an unwanted bramble.

The building is dominated by a large central chimney stack, shared by the two middle dwellings. Those at the ends have later and smaller chimneys of their own, each with two fireplaces, one up, one down. During the Victorian rebuilding, each household also acquired a brick extension for a kitchen and bedroom at the back. You can see these additions at the ends of the terrace from the way the slope of the roof near the bottom changes its angle and becomes a little shallower in a characteristic Suffolk way. On a similar long-house a few yards down the road from ours, the roof extends at the back right down to shoulder height, giving a strikingly unbroken expanse of pantiles from end to end of the building.

The most striking features of the whole terrace are the jazzy eyebrows over the windows, simply but efficiently cut from quite intricately-shaped lengths of wood which drips can run off, and the four porches, one over each door. These flamboyant items and particularly the curvy diagonals that support their roofs, were inventively designed, with chamfered columns tapering upwards and a scalloped barge-boarded roof over them. The perspective along the four pairs of them spread across the length of the whole longhouse justifies the trouble they must have been to make. The four solid front doors were elegantly thought-up too, each with four recessed panels, semicircular at the top. Someone must have worked this out carefully and not scrimped. Nature, or the gardening, has done its bit too in the growth around the hexagonal wooden columns. These had rotted at base and had to be renewed, a task that seemed simple enough but involved carefully copying unsuspected subtleties in the detailing of the chamfering and the shapes of the scalloped edges. When it's warm the door stays open most of the time. The flowerbed beside it is home to field mice and shrews and is the first place our cat makes for each time we arrive.

From outside, the house looks quite orderly. But inside, it seems
more haphazard. You can see how the original building was
constructed from the substantial remnants or outcrops of the old
structural timbers in key uprights and beams. There are cool brick
floors downstairs, of a pale creamy colour and laid in a simple
consistent pattern. The house unusually has a cellar, also dark and
cool; sometimes newts get into it. There are lots of doors except
between the two houses No.1 and No.2, and a number of small
bedrooms upstairs and in the attic. The upstairs ceilings droop
and sag languorously and I enjoy drawing them.

The house is at its best in spring and summer, and on other
unexpectedly sunny days when it's warmer out than in. Through
the door are reminders of when tennis was played on a neighbour's
court by us and more recently by our children. The small oil
painting above the chair is of a Scottish landscape by my mother;
there are other paintings by her and my father throughout the
house, and also some Victorian and more recent prints.

In the back kitchen of No.2 cottage survive several items now becoming rare – a cast-iron kitchen range, still perfect in all its intricate detail, and an old-fashioned copper, the shape of a kettle-drum, over its own fireplace which heated up the water. The copper was heavily patched and riveted together during its hard-worked past, and now looks like the copper-bottomed hull of a clipper; we keep sticks for kindling in it. An old oblong Belfast sink also survives in situ; there is another outside in the garden, full of plants. Although this room is still called a kitchen, it's really just a vital extra space for mainly outdoor activities, a chilly no-man's land, half in, half out. The outer door is thick and heavy and in two halves like a stable door. Most of the interior doors however are merely a few planks, simpler and thinner and far from soundproof. The door latches, bolts and hinges throughout have the quirky knocked-off individuality that comes from having been made by a busy village blacksmith.

The wood burner at the bottom of the big central chimney occupies a large recess which projects into our neighbour's side-room. The most memorable beam in the house is the one over the fireplace recess that now houses the wood burner. This great beam has a number of merchant marks incised into it, probably sixteenth century and including a consecration mark made up of three connecting circles, supposedly to ward off the evil eye. The flue goes straight up and has a splendid draught, so lighting a fire is never a problem, but after seeing to the fire I often bang my head on this beam. The heavy oak upright projecting from the wall to the left of the door (opposite) supports a cross-beam in the ceiling. With your back to the woodburner you can see through a small study into the room where we eat if there are too many people for the kitchen table and it's too cold for the garden.

Sometimes jackdaws build nests on the chimneys and occasionally fall down inside them. Once when we had been away for a week or two we returned to find one dead on the floor; a moment later we found its mate, exhausted and starving but still able to hop feebly about in the next room. We gave it some food and opened the door and it just managed to flap unsteadily away.

Upstairs the floor timbers are of oak – wide boards, dark, uneven and creaky – and the upstairs fireplaces are of Victorian cast iron, black and ornate and possibly local – there is still a working foundry about fifteen miles away. In the two main bedrooms the ceilings sag quite dramatically; the one in No.2 also creaks when our neighbours move about overhead, where their attic overhangs our bedroom in a way not uncommon in Suffolk.

We bought the chairs and tables and iron bedsteads cheaply from local sales or auctions while these still existed. Otherwise we have left everything pretty much as it was, altering the structure and even the decoration of the house as little as possible and retaining some unassuming old wallpapers. We have also kept the old electrics – wiring, switches and switchboxes – and haven't installed central heating, which we thought would dry out and endanger the whole structure of the building.

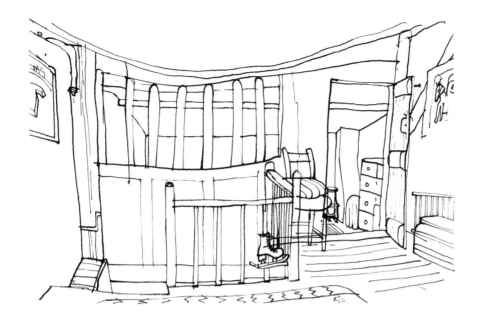

Part of the interest of drawing inside a house full of small rooms is the open-door perspectives they afford through intervening rooms only the size of a closet or squashed upstairs in the attic into the space left beside the central chimney's flue. The stairs are steep and narrow, and the carpenters were skillful at squeezing cramped and steep staircases into the corners of already small rooms. One bedroom (above) still includes the much older wooden frame of an outside window left over from the time before the back extension was added but now opening instead into another tiny bedroom. The views from room to room (overleaf) are complicated by mirrors which reflect the room behind one as well. The harvest lithograph is by John Nash.

The building's most striking decorative features, seen from both inside and out, are its window frames. Uniform throughout like the porches and the doors, they would have been the work of Victorian estate carpenters or joiners. The frames are chamfered consistently throughout the whole building, making the windows look more delicate within and without and also letting more light into the rooms.

The attic is divided in two by a chimney flue, with on one side another small bedroom, reached up wooden stairs so steep that a rope handrail is needed, and on the other by what used to be a children's playroom, full of boxes of books, a wooden fort, dolls, and ancient tin trunks. The attic is the right size for children, who can't yet bang their heads on the ceiling.

The house has one feature unusual in this region: a cellar, chilly and reached by some steep and cramped wooden steps, and inhabited intermittently by newts and toads. There is a tiny window and a small drain hole in one corner which these creatures used to fall into and then couldn't get out. We used to find their dried-up husks until we built a wooden ramp for them to climb out.

garden

The garden when we arrived was tidy in front but a mess at the back. The house faces south, so the front garden is sunny and in warm weather it becomes an extra room. Its lawn is good for deck-chairs and rugs for our children, exhausted first by school exams and now by their jobs, and for our young grandchildren as a place to leave bikes and games and occasionally dig holes.

We can all eat out under the apple tree. Here, since it's easy to imagine ourselves unseen from the road, we enjoy a sense of privacy. This is an illusion; the garden hedge must be for passers-by merely an interestingly thin screen but is for us a notional protection only, with its thin patches and holes easier to see through than we might imagine. We in turn can enjoy views across hedge and road and through another hedge to the pheasants, pigeons, partridges and hares on the field beyond. In mid-winter a great flock of fieldfares sometimes unexpectedly settle there to feed for a few hours before moving on en masse, leaving no stragglers behind. In the garden behind the house, the children can play croquet and badminton, climb bigger trees and look into our neighbours' gardens. To our cat, the garden's hedges mean exercise, rejuvenation and fun as she changes from being a radiator-hugging London layabout into a lithe and ruthless hunter.

The garden is divided into three separate bits, two in front and one at the back. The narrow patch in front of No.2 is left to its own devices, self-seeded and lovely in spring when the crocuses, snowdrops, and daffodils are out. In summer it becomes a deep grassy jungle almost hiding the white gate onto the road. Its role is more to be looked at and drawn than trodden on.

My parents liked gardening, but apart from lighting and tending bonfires, I didn't much. But seeing this garden develop with its flower beds, herb garden and small vegetable patch is like watching someone grow up. What we inherited in it were pear, damson, bullace and cherry trees, and various mature apple trees. We also once bought some young fruit trees and planted the oak sapling which is now a small tree that wood-pigeons nest in; the thick but low hedge underneath it separates the two front gardens.

The main garden in front of No.1 is bigger and much more used. The apple trees in the corner nearest the road were already propped up when we arrived, and still subside a bit and grow more horizontal every year, but their crop of good yellow apples remains steady. When it's warm we set up a trestle table in their shade for lunch, and hang a hammock between them in which our children can go to sleep. This bit of the garden is mostly lawn, though there is a narrow and beautiful flower-bed between the front door and the garden gate. As well as the apple trees there is a crab apple hung with bird-feeders, a hawthorn, a laburnum and some bits of lilac. On the far side of the road there was always a gap in the hedge which Sue discreetly enlarged so that she could watch hares boxing in the field beyond. This hole has since grown bigger still of its own accord as the small elm saplings that previously framed it have themselves withered and died, leaving only bare branches which blackbirds perch on and woodpeckers bore into. The drawing overleaf shows how it looks now.

A proper snowfall is sometimes preceded by a light frosty dusting of snow on the lawn but not deep enough to fill the furrows in the field. In winter everything is easier to see into – other gardens, the structure of the inside of hedges. The bare branches of the oak tree make a roughly triangular composition with our neighbours' white end wall, something I'd not noticed before. When the heavy snow comes it makes everything silent and almost black-and-white. The birds, quite well camouflaged against brown backgrounds, now stand out clearly against the whiteness. As a boy I already liked a Brueghel painting of a winter scene with its brilliant contrasts of black and white, and unidentifiable birds in the bare trees against the greys of sky and distant frozen ponds and hunters setting out in the snow. Every snowfall still makes me think of him. In winter when it's too cold to work outside I draw the views from the upstairs windows onto the garden and the trees and fields beyond the hedge. The cat sits on the window ledge beside me, looking down on the crab apple tree with its flutter of blue tits and goldfinches, fierce and bold at this time of year, and mews with frustration at their inaccessibility. She has never caught a bird.

The front lawn squeezes past the end of the house and then opens
out again behind it as a long grassy stretch leading to a narrow
brook which serves as a natural boundary. There is a beautifully
lichened brick wall which would have been built for the old rectory
next door. Against it grow comfrey, nettles and ivy. This bit of the
garden must also once have been a rubbish tip, for at the foot of
the wall are bricks, bits of broken glass, big flints and other stones,
and tree roots; I once saw a slow worm, a small legless lizard there.

    The back garden behind the house is different in character from
the front – longer, more open and almost like a small field. It is
flanked by other very dissimilar gardens – the old rectory's with its
small lake, croquet lawn and many big trees, and the narrower plots
of our neighbours on the other side, which are tended in various
ways, decorative or practical. Looking down on it from our attic
window I can see the garden shed, the apple trees in the distance,
the lake next door and the big chestnuts beside it.

When we arrived, the garden at the back of the house was dauntingly neglected and overgrown. We got a tractor to clear the undergrowth away and give it a rough dig, and then with Sue's father's help dug and raked it ourselves in preparation for sowing with the mixture of clover and grass seed that he gave us. It was a memorable task that everyone in the family joined in, broadcasting the seed by hand, then rolling the tilth, and finally pushing in lots of sticks with silvery plastic streamers in an attempt to keep the birds away from the seeds. On this bit of the garden there were already several mature and twisted apple trees, a cherry tree, a spiny bullace, a damson and a greengage; some of these have died but the younger ones remain, to be pruned, harvested and climbed on. The garden has been well used by children and grandchildren and I enjoy drawing it. The view looking back up the garden from the stream shows the projecting Victorian kitchens. The top drawing on the left was made when there were more swallows and martins to sit on the electric wires and the telegraph pole was surrounded by its clump of ferns and hops. The one below shows our garden shed with its thinning elder.

The back shed is full of well-used old garden tools bought at auctions or car boot sales. Spades, trowels, and rakes and forks hang from nails on its walls. Such familiar objects look simple and plain, but they are complex in shape and harder to draw than they appear because everyone knows what they look like. Eric Ravilious drew such tools affectionately and accurately. There are other items – a boot scraper and a garden roller with a makers' nameplate on its handle – which, being of cast iron, are indestructible. Admittedly the wooden part of the roller's handle has rotted away, but from the side it still embodies the idea of the well-kept garden which ours certainly isn't. But although I'm generally assigned undemanding tasks like apple picking, nettle cutting, raking leaves and carting wheelbarrow loads to compost heap or bonfire, I enjoy these activities and feeling useful around the place instead of only ever looking at the garden for things to draw, like the honeysuckle over the arch where our cat hides in wait longing to catch sparrows.

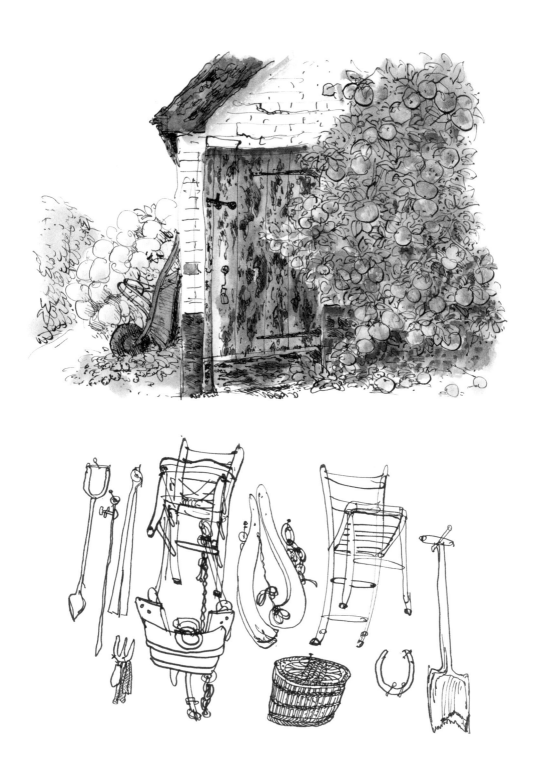

The elder tree behind the shed was much climbed in by the children and at first it flourished. It was very beautiful when its flowers were out, catching as much of the sunlight as they could by spreading out, curving round and thus emphasising the shape and beauty of the tree. I tried to keep it healthy by pruning out its rampaging green suckers but in the end it was pulled down by age and ivy and it died away altogether. It used to have the disintegrating remains of a water butt at its base, just held in shape by its rusty hoops. I had liked elder bushes as a boy, trying to make whistles out of their hollowed-out sticks and on sunny days using a magnifying glass to set alight bits of their dried pith.

This corner of the back garden was always tempting to draw, with the patterns of the S-shaped pantiles on this side of the longhouse and on the sheds, in contrast to the flat plaintiles of the front roof. The shed is surrounded by ferns and cow parsley and long grasses and also by the bric-a-brac of a garden, which are given a certain charm merely by having turned back from discardable rubbish into useful and durable relics.

In the thirty-odd years since we came here the garden has changed quite a lot. Some of the trees, like the bullace with its yellow heartwood, have simply died; others have been trimmed back by the electricity supply company; new apples and pears and an oak tree have been planted; a climbing frame and a swing have come and gone as the needs of children and grandchildren have developed. I like pruning the apple trees and picking the apples, greengages and pears; dead-heading the evening primroses in early autumn; pulling up nettles and dead cow-parsley; lighting and tending bonfires. I enjoyed for a while the friendly company of our neighbours' hen and admire the cat's prowess in catching small animals while hating her subsequent tossing, re-catching and killing (though never eating) them. Most of all I like watching our grandchildren playing in the garden, climbing trees or turning cartwheels and somersaults on the grass, in their headlong rush through what seems to me their brief childhood.

Early on during our time here the cow parsley which seeded itself at the far end of the garden looked lovely in spring under the apple, cherry and hawthorn blossom, so apart from an access path mown down to the stream we at first left this area untouched. But the resulting wilderness re-seeded itself with new intensity every year and became more and more uncontrollable, beautiful in May but an unkempt mess later on, so it now gets mown several times a year. But at the very end of the garden we have gone on letting docks, nettles and comfrey grow every summer to discourage grandchildren from getting too easily into the stream. Here the garden becomes a wilder place. Wood pigeons nest in the hawthorn clumps by the water's edge and we find the white shells of their eggs lying on the grass nearby, apparently whole but disappointingly empty, dropped there by jays or magpies that had raided the nest. Grass snakes used to live in the shady and inaccessible bit under this hawthorn. Once I saw some baby snakes there; another time I spotted a fully-grown one half-hidden in the dark undergrowth nearby, eyeing me as motionlessly as I was watching it, until after a while I realised it wasn't a real snake at all but just its sloughed-off skin. We hung it up from the mantelpiece but it tended to upset visitors.

Birds are the most vital and pervasive wild presence around us –
coming as confidently as if invited to the bird-feeders in the crab
apple tree, flitting and whirring about just outside the window;
hopping or running on the lawn like the blackbirds and crows;
picking their way stealthily like the moorhens or stalking fearless
and proprietorial like the cock pheasant. There are fewer swallows
and house martins than there used to be, and others like willow
warblers, cuckoos and flycatchers we no longer see or hear at all.
We hear ducks and moorhens in the stream and in our neighbours'
lake. For a while we also enjoyed the visits of one of our neighbours'
chickens, a friendly and privileged one which followed us (or
indeed anyone) about, eating from our hands and pecking
hopefully at jeans and wellies. She had the run of all the nearby
gardens until she ate too many seedlings and was put back with
her friends in the chicken-run.

In contrast with the birds, most of the wild animals one sees around here however are already dead – the badgers, hares, muntjacs and hedgehogs that we see lying whole or squashed at the edge of the road. There are also the moles, mice, small voles and shrews that our cat catches, brings in, torments, tosses about, loses and then forgets. But the garden is also unobtrusively frequented by muntjacs, rabbits, rats, mice and voles; and more secretively by moles, grass snakes, newts and occasional toads and frogs. We have seen foxes, rats and weasels or stoats running across the lane and a water vole in the stream. On the field in front of the house as well as the crows, pigeons and pheasants we see hares boxing, pheasants and, until quite recently, hedgehogs, but the ones we used to see in the garden at dusk, sniffing about by the hedge, have stopped coming and must all have been run over, or perhaps just be dying out. Sometimes when I'm sitting in a field drawing, a hare will come quite near, seem not to notice me and lope off again into the standing corn paying no attention. Sue once found an unsquashed hare lying on a grassy bank by the roadside. She skinned it and made a delicious-looking dish of jugged hare; we tried to eat it but it wasn't much good.

Stream

The stream at the foot of our garden flows between steep banks and is shaded on our side by hawthorns and elder bushes. In spring it is a pretty rivulet, too wide and inaccessible here to jump across and just too deep for even adults' gumboots. In dry summers it becomes an unprepossessing dry ditch where our grandchildren find rusty iron bedsteads, stoneware jars and bottles and fragments of not very old pottery. But in winter or after heavy rain it regularly but briefly becomes a quite impressive brown torrent. I have only once seen fish in it but there are wild ducks on the water, moorhens pick their way about at the far end of the garden, and we have found newts – even crested ones – nearby; geese from the lake downstream fly overhead, we have occasionally seen a heron and, just once, a kingfisher.

On the far side of the stream a footpath follows its course upstream, past a plantation of young saplings, beside old oak trees and between cornfields, grassy meadows and horse gallops. Upstream still further it narrows and eventually dwindles away to little more than a ditch. Downstream, the path leads through a leafy tunnel of hornbeams called the Causeway into the village. A little further on the stream flows into the River Blyth which ten miles further on still, at Blythburgh, becomes the Blyth estuary.

The walk upstream on the far side of the stream is lovely. Some of the overhanging trees, like the hornbeams and beeches, have smooth bark; others like the oaks are textured, others striated and fissured. Old oak trees can become almost overwhelmed by heavy ivy which gives them striking silhouettes but will eventually do them in. It's harder to notice in summer when everything is green, but in winter it gives a different shape, aspect and silhouette to the aged tree.

I realised how imperceptibly a ditch becomes a stream while making a drawing where a grassy footpath crossed over a field drain. The ditch, here hardly more than a groove between overgrown banks, is fed by the sloping fields at either side, and then itself feeds in turn into our own stream, a bigger but still nameless tributary of the River Blyth. In early April it is bordered but not overgrown by last year's dried grasses and you can still see water gleaming beneath them. But already the main stream a few hundred yards away is almost invisible beneath longer grass and sparkling blackthorn blossom.

The stream is a beautiful but perplexing subject to draw. Upstream it thins and flows between grassy banks and in winter it's easy to follow its curving course. When it floods, after prolonged rain or when snow melts, it's quite alarming. In early May blackthorn blossom and catkins screen it from the nearby road and even from the footpath that runs beside it. Spring growth hides it in the tunnelled woodland stretches, turning it into a kind of mossy and mysterious jungle. In summer it becomes so overgrown as to be almost invisible, until when you've forgotten it's there at all it suddenly gleams out at you between the tree trunks or dazzlingly reflects a low sun. Later on the stream more or less dries up; in winter when it snows the water seems almost black by contrast with all the whiteness around it. I try drawing it quickly or more carefully in various media, with pencils and bold graphite sticks, marker pens and felt-tips, and then with a dipping-pen and watercolour, each time trying to suggest a different aspect of it but of course never sure how each drawing will work out. Only later can I tell which drawings I quite like, which not much or not at all. Water is a tantalising subject to draw anyway, whether it's a lake or a puddle.

Towards the village the stream runs from our garden along between steep banks with the road on one side and the Causeway, an artificial raised track, on the other. The path along the causeway is flanked by two rows of hornbeams which in summer form a leafy tunnel and in winter a complicated tracery of interlocking branches. It is beautiful at all seasons – in wintry mist when the path through it vanishes into a hazy distance; in spring when it sparkles with catkins and bright new opening buds; in summer (overleaf) when it is dark and heavy but with shafts of sunlight breaking through gaps in the foliage. In autumn it is rich with fungi, the ground is yellow with fallen leaves, and the shadows of the trees fall across the sloping banks and the path, revealing more clearly the causeway's underlying shape. Many of the hornbeams are in clumps sprung from the stumps of old trees which have been cut short or pollarded. After a light snowfall the scene looks magical, with the successive clumps and stumps of hornbeams fading into the distance and the path trodden by only a few walkers beside the newly snow-darkened stream.

Bits of the stream are tucked away, screened by impenetrable undergrowth and bramble thickets and hard to get at down its steep or slippery banks. You are sometimes hardly aware of the presence of water until you suddenly notice the reflections of sun or sky glinting through a screen of foliage and ivy-covered tree trunks. These add variety and a change from the smooth hornbeams which don't seem to attract ivy. The far side of the stream is hidden by its own thick roadside hedges.

There are prettier, shallower and more accessible bits of the stream further down the causeway; they are also the most beautiful. These were the first parts of the stream our children knew and liked best. When they were small, someone hung a strong rope from an upper branch so that the village children – of whom there were then more – could swing across from side to side of the stream, just missing the water, which anyway was shallow enough there to paddle in. This kept the bottom of the stream clean and pebbly and good to look at, even in summer when the water level was low.

Most of the older hornbeams along the causeway have been
pollarded, with their trunks cut off about two metres from the
ground so that their shoots would quickly grow into thinner
branches that could be cut for firewood. This second growth often
spreads out like a Y. The sloping branches and trunks form a series
of triangular arches for one to walk through. Pollarding is just
pruning – a poll meant a head, as in poll tax, and pollarded meant
cropped short, as if in a haircut. The shoots, desperate for light,
grow in snaky curves, but the original trunk grows instead into
strange lumps and in time the tree itself often hollows out. When
a hornbeam grows old its trunk often splits apart, revealing the
contorted hollow interior. The stumps too look bent and stressed,
as if even now they are still straining and twisting. These low trunks
are easily climbed and hidden or picnicked in, as our children and
grandchildren quickly discovered. Hornbeam timber is very hard
and the tree is sometimes called ironwood; its wood was used in the
past as gear-wheel pegs in windmills, for chess pieces and in pianos
for the levers that make the hammers hit the strings. Oaks too split
open when very old, like the gesturing one on the right, further
down the causeway where the hornbeams thin out.

The causeway is beautiful in spring, with thin still semi-transparent foliage, many of the older tree trunks on either side of the path growing out sideways at surprisingly steep angles. When the sun shines, their snaky shoots and branches cast shadows that reveal the shape and section of the causeway, something that on a grey day is not so clear. You can see the way the roots protect the sloping surfaces of the banks from disintegrating and also the ditch and farm track on the far side and the plantation beside and below it. For a week or two in May the trees in the coppice below seem to rise out of a wonderful waist-high sea of blossoming cow parsley. In summer the central pathway along the causeway becomes a stately and romantic avenue; occasionally there used to be glow-worms. In winter on a grey night without starlight it becomes quite alarming because you can't see where you're going and unseen branches brush your face.

When drawing the causeway on a sunny winter's day, its main
elements – trees, path, stream, even the surrounding landscape –
are all in clear view. On one side the central track tilts slightly towards
the stream and then drops steeply down into it; on the other side,
a secondary and slightly higher ridge carries another row of snaky
trees and then drops down sharply into a narrow field drain, with
a cart track beyond it. In spring and summer, these slopes are partly
hidden under longer grasses and undergrowth.

Late one afternoon when I was drawing in the causeway there
were only a few passers-by, mostly walking dogs, but one was a mother
whose daughter was almost but not quite able to ride her bike unaided.
I remembered as a boy being at this on-the-brink stage and then
suddenly sensing that no one was running behind me holding the
bike upright; and all these years later enjoying my children's and now
grandchildren's delight when as if magically they could do it too.

Further downstream the banks are steeper; you need to hang onto branches or tree trunks or their roots to get down to the water and back up again. The opposite bank, which supports the road, is steeper still and less accessible, and in places it has needed concrete sandbags to shore it up. The trees on either side of the stream lean over and across it, tangling in a cat's-cradle of trunks and branches, some of them thick with creepers. The tree trunks are dark themselves, and black-leaved creepers make them look darker still. You can see the bottom of the stream only where a reflection of something dark crosses it; elsewhere, you see only the dazzling reflection of the sky, which overpowers anything darker. Where the stream is at its deepest it tunnels through a forest of overhanging branches. If you stand on the bank and look back up the stream, you can see the inverted reflections of trees more clearly than the confusing and hard-to-disentangle reality above them.

The trees slope across stream, causeway and drain, creating tunnels of trunks and foliage. From time to time some of them, hornbeams and oaks alike, fall across the stream or the path. Usually they pull their shallow roots up with them, and even when the fallen trunks have been sawn up and carted off the exposed roots tend to be left behind, still tilted at a crazy angle but eventually becoming a permanent part of the scene. Even as mossy and splintered stumps the hornbeams still retain their twisty vigour. In summer the crumbling banks are covered with ferns and soft, cushiony mosses, and it's harder to see down to the sandy bottom of the stream. In autumn fungi appear on the ground and inside the hollow trunks. As the causeway approaches the village, its rural character changes: gardens appear on the opposite side of the stream, shoring up their banks with elaborate wooden or concrete esplanades and steps.

Village

The village lies in a shallow valley amid rich farming country. It has two distinct parts, a mile apart from each other and quite dissimilar. The newer bit clusters around a triangular village green where three roads meet, and consists of the pub and its outbuildings, the village hut, and a number of houses – some handsome, others just old, still others interesting or picturesque or good of their kind, some nondescript. Two of the houses are again in classic Suffolk longhouse style – wide and timber-framed, with a pantiled roof, well-spaced windows, and wicket fencing separating them from the road. There is also a post-war council estate and an enclave of recently built executive-type brick houses.

The other and older part of the village comprises the church, its original rectory standing in its own small park, a pretty Victorian school and schoolhouse, and two more longhouses, our own and another. The two bits of the village reflect their past significance in the life of the village – the populous and domestic part near the village green, and the once more formal functions of church, rectory and school. These separate parts are linked by a shaded and pretty lane, running beside the stream. To either side of this stretch fields which slope upwards to skylines about half a mile away and help to keep off the biting Suffolk wind.

The modest village hut, a wooden building by the green, is unassuming and picturesquely bendy but undeniably run-down. Parish meetings and social occasions are held there, and there has been much discussion about how ambitiously or affordably the hut should be renewed and what new form it should take. For the present the pub provides a more active social centre. The Huntingfield Arms is a well-proportioned building, with the coat of arms painted on a board over the door. Its tables and benches spread out on to the green, along with the cast iron remains of an old pump and a war memorial. On summer days the green becomes a pleasantly informal village centre itself. On its far side where there used to be a sandpit is a small car park and a children's playground, and on the higher ground beyond this, up some wooden steps, is the Millennium Green, used for sports and occasional cricket matches. When we first came here there was a group of youngish hippies living in the row of cottages by the village bridge who made big one-off inflatables, their dinosaurs and coloured octopi swaying in the Easter breeze as they were tested out on the green. Nowadays in summer people gather there before going on bird-watching walks or to enjoy folk dancing.

The village post office had shut just before we came here and is now remembered only because of its name on the wall of the house where it used to be. Other reminders of an earlier village life remain in the names of other houses and cottages – the Old Forge, Laundry Cottage, Malt Terrace, Church Terrace, plus a number with less convincing or more wistful names and also the tautologous Thatched Cottage. There are in fact three thatched buildings in the village, the hall of the old school and two small cottages, but the most common local roofs are of pantiles or plain tiles, their flatter and simpler variants. The prettiest row of cottages, in summer at least, is the most ordinary – the Victorian red-brick row by the small bridge across the stream at the end of the causeway. The brickwork of the bridge has a cast iron coping, like several others in nearby villages. Other houses are individual and inventive, and mostly painted white, cream/yellow or pink. Beside the pub is its small, old and rickety-looking wooden barn with a picturesquely sagging roof. The most unified group of buildings are the council houses on Holland Rise, set back from the road and well designed and maintained.

As you walk up from the centre of the village towards the other part around the church, the old trees that overhang the road form a kind of Gothic tunnel and hide the church itself. The first building you see is the old school, its thatched roof and pointed gables echoing in shape the trees that frame it. The schoolroom, the original and central part of the school, is tall and has beautiful and intricate barge boards above a finely-carved decorative window frame. The school has a lovely garden whose gate is directly opposite the gate into the churchyard. For much of our time there the organist, who was also a fine violinist, lived in the school with her husband, a musical administrator who had previously been a singer.

On the higher land around the village are scattered isolated cottages and farms, mostly attractive without being surprising, but including three that stand out. One is ancient and Dutch-looking, another apparently Regency and very pretty, and the last a remarkably adventurous twenty-first century structure. These, and the oaks in the fields, are the village's real landmarks.

From the higher ground beyond the village, the very close grouping
of church and rectory is striking, with the tower of one and the
rebuilt façade of the other separated (if you stand in the right
place) by a tall chestnut tree. For distant views of the village you
have to climb these slopes, though even then you seldom see more
than chimneys and isolated gables. But from higher up still there
are wonderful views of the surrounding countryside, on which are
several isolated farmhouses, some distant church towers and a
handsome eighteenth century mansion.

Apart from its extraordinary painted roof the church is modest
in size and interest. But from close at hand, surrounded by its lush
graveyard with some interesting gravestones and beautiful trees,
it is very pretty. The churchyard is surrounded by trees and full of
old gravestones in front; more recent ones are round at the back.
I enjoy wandering about among the older ones, comparing their
sometimes quite complicated shapes and reading the names on
them, some touching, others slightly comic. I like the place best
when it's not looking too tidy.

The church tower is rather severe, apart from its battlements, but it has a beautiful porch, of ashlar and knapped flint, with a small sundial on it and a complicated interplay of flint in repeat patterns and slight changes of plane where the buttresses jut out at an angle. The porch has a beautiful wavy pattern at the top: quite difficult to draw, as is the whole design of the porch, because if you get one proportion wrong you put the whole thing out of joint – lines just don't meet. One way to tackle this is to look for a portion of it which seems roughly square (like the central arch together with all the panels to its right) and then build the rest on to that square.

St Mary's Huntingfield is partly late medieval, with a handsome but battered font and two perpendicular windows. There are some fragments of medieval glass (appropriately of hunting dogs and hares) in the south aisle, and a fine peal of five bells in the tower. The church was much rebuilt in the eighteenth century and has many very interesting seventeenth and eighteenth century monuments on the walls and set into the floor, and from the nineteenth century a brass lectern and an intricate font cover of wood. The remarkable painted ceiling is a monument to the dedication and determination of Mildred Holland who between 1859 and 1866, lying on her back and without any help, covered every inch of it with paintings of saints and angels, separated by heraldic-looking patterns on the diagonal roof beams. Mildred was the wife of the rich rector, the Reverend William Holland, who outlived her by twenty years. Maybe she had been worn out by her task.

The church is also interesting for the twelve brightly-coloured and boldly-carved wooden angels, wings outstretched, that look down on the normally empty nave below. When the church is lit from the inside, as on a dark winter afternoon, the painted roof, the gilded angels and the painted structure of the window at the east end sparkle and glitter in an entirely Victorian way, at odds with

the severe wall plaques and the crude but vigorous monumental slabs on the floor, the beautiful medieval porch and font, and the austere square tower outside. The Christmas carol service seems Victorian too – the conventions, tunes and words that remind me of the daily assembly at my school when these rituals, since there were none at home, were new and strange to me. The tunes and the singing are still touching but the words of the service have too many incredible things requiring to be believed in. The small door into the spiral staircase is now kept locked, but when it was still open I liked climbing up to the belfry with our son, seeing the bells and looking down into the nave. I admire the bell ringers' energy and interdependence and they don't seem to mind being drawn.

Half-hidden just behind the church is the old rectory, a handsome building of Suffolk white brick. Its domain includes a small park surrounded by pretty iron chain-link fencing and a garden with a lake in the woodland just beyond our own garden wall, the whole embodying the comfortable social standing of the established church in Victorian times. Behind the rectory is a wooden tithe barn, and there are fine horse chestnut trees and a croquet lawn within a clipped yew hedge. Of the whole complex of church, school house, old rectory (and its red-brick 1950s replacement) and the two supposedly associated longhouses, none any longer retains its original function or significance in village life. Even the church, despite its architectural and historical interest, is empty for most of the time, apart from occasional harvest festivals, weddings, funerals, bell-ringings, exhibitions of paintings and photographs, and Christmas and Easter services for small and mostly elderly congregations. The two nearby longhouses, thought to have belonged initially to the church and previously occupied by craftsmen and farmworkers, are now – like most of the village's houses – owned by relatively recent outsiders like us. Two exceptions are our next door neighbours in Church Terrace. When we came both of them still worked on the village's one big farm.

High House Farm lies about a mile west of Huntingfield on the high ground towards Laxfield and is wholly surrounded by farmland. It is of red brick and distinguished by the splendidly flamboyant Dutch gables on its front and sides. Apart from the church it is the oldest building anywhere near the village and dates itself 1700 on its own brickwork. The style of the gables reflects the region's eighteenth century trading relationship with the Low Countries just across the sea. It is still a working farm, currently half-screened behind its own trees and barns, and run by a friendly and communicative farmer.

The footpath from the village that runs in front of the farm also takes you past Huntingfields' newest house, an intriguing structure remarkable for its outer barn-like wooden shell which can be slid back and forth to reveal or conceal the glazed interior. A wind turbine helps to move it to and fro. When I drew it the owners had just been cutting their own hay, which lay drying before it in softly curving swathes.

Huntingfield Hall, the village's prettiest building, stands on the slope a little to the north of the village and in full and artfully contrived view of Heveningham Hall, for whose delectation this previously unremarkable farmhouse was transformed in the late eighteenth century into a delightful eye-catcher by adding on an intricately designed Gothic revival façade. Nearby oaks frame it and screen the view of the farm buildings behind it. In front of it beyond a ha-ha stand the still vigorous remains of the Queen's Oak, under which Queen Elizabeth I is supposed to have killed a stag. Sheep sometimes graze around this tree and if they're there when it snows they continue to sit patiently and picturesquely on, as if in a chilly but romantic idyll. Its owner, who had grown up in the big Hall, later lived in this smaller one and farmed the land around it. When our children were young she held an annual open day at lambing time, with treasure hunts for the children (the prize buried in a sand-tray – you had to stick a stake in where you thought it was hidden) and for the grown-ups raffles, bowling for the pig, second-hand books, homemade cakes and prize vegetables, the village's teas and scones, and her own welcoming and gently patrician presence.

The oldest of the many oaks around the village is the Queen's Oak. It looks less ruined, neglected and abandoned than it did twenty years ago and is now repaired and cared for and protected from sheep by a pretty iron railing. Its trunk stands far to one side of its remaining branches, giving it from front and back a remarkable asymmetry, as if it might topple over (from the sides it looks perfectly stable). The views from it emphasise the intimate connection between nearby Huntingfield Hall and Heveningham Hall in the distance.

The trunk also presents two very different facets, the side nearest Huntingfield Hall though lumpy and distorted still retaining most of its bark (overleaf), the other side looking riven and blasted and ripped savagely apart or dismembered. There are other fine oaks nearby, unravished by time and splendidly sited on the crest of a grassy ridge overlooking the widened-out valley of the Blyth.

An oak surrounded by sheep is a familiar symbol of rural well-being. Mature oaks have a thickset sturdiness not unlike that of the Suffolk Punch horse. The oak tree has long been a potent national symbol of strength and endurance. So when selecting two motifs for a sign for the village that would symbolise its history, rural character and name, I chose the Queen's Oak together with one of the hares which used to be hunted here and are still often seen in the surrounding fields.

Huntingfield

Hall

The dominant architectural feature of the surrounding landscape is Heveningham Hall. From the road, the north side of the hall itself looks quite severe, its long flat skyline enlivened only by pediments and a central coat of arms. But the dark stucco of this splendid but chilly-looking façade is transformed around midsummer when the evening sun reaches it and it glows golden against the large dark trees behind it. The view it looks out on, which one can see from the footpath in front of the hall, is magnificent – a gleaming lake through which flows our anonymous village stream, now joined by the main River Blyth. The ground rises beyond it and hides the cars on the Walpole road – tall pedestrians on this road have the best distant views of the hall. The footpath leads one back to the road across a new Palladian bridge. Beyond the road the ground slopes up across a wide pasture with many oaks and sheep to the belt of woodland on the skyline. The hidden south front of the hall, which one can see on the two days of its summer Country Fair, is less forbidding and lighter in colour than the north, and faces a remarkable amphitheatre of grass terraces. Beyond this on the crest of the slope are a rococo orangery, some fine cedars and a well-restored walled garden, its plants and vegetables laid out with skill and imagination within a crinkle-crankle wall.

Heveningham Hall was built in 1778-84 by Sir Robert Taylor with interiors by James Wyatt. The classic views of it are from the Walpole road on the north, across the lake created by widening the River Blyth. This parkland landscaping is a late work by the great 18th century master Capability Brown. But his plans to widen the stream beyond the bridge were never realised and when I first saw the hall the main lake was silting up and the stream towards Walpole was narrow. Under its present owner Brown's original plans have now been implemented and taken further by the landscape designer Kim Wilkie. The main lake has been dredged and restored, and the Blyth widened downstream beyond a new bridge to form the second lake that Brown had proposed but could not carry out. Broadleaf trees are being planted on every skyline visible from the hall.

On the field opposite the hall are collected piles of wood which every November 5th become a huge bonfire. If one is standing near the bonfire one can see it reflected in the windows of the distant Hall, which seems for a instant itself to be on fire. When the park is under snow the hall's grey stucco façade seems by contrast to turn almost black. It looks at its most magnificent late on a summer's day when the sun has reached round to enliven its long and splendid façade. The rush-fringed lake (overleaf) is especially beautiful under changeable summer skies.

The hall looks good at all seasons, in very varied lights and from many different standpoints. Its appearance depends heavily on where the sun is, or on grey days whether it's dry or overcast or misty or snowy (overleaf) and whether or not the trees in front of it are in leaf and what's in the way. The central and most obvious views from directly in front of the hall are partly screened by old oaks, clumps of alder and recently planted willows. Quick on-the-spot sketches help me to work out the pros and cons of different viewpoints. The Halesworth road in front of the hall is quite busy, yet once when I was walking along its narrow grass verge by the railings in search of the best view a wild duck flew up as I almost trod on her nest full of grey-green eggs.

The recreation of Capability Brown's designs and principles, seen in the restored shape of the previously silting-up lake, required the intensive use of earth-moving equipment supposedly left over from the channel tunnel.

Every summer a Country Fair is held here, with sheepdog trials, demonstrations of birds of prey, shows of llamas and camels, rabbits and poultry. There are rallies of traction engines and tractors, vintage planes and helicopter trips. The fair gives one a chance to see at close range the Hall and its gardens, orangery and magnificent tiltyard. Then in November there are fireworks and a big bonfire on the field beyond the lake.

A beautiful and traditional element in the parkland landscape is the flock of sheep that graze in it. They have been looked after by a succession of shepherds and their dogs. For a while, one of them lived in Huntingfield Hall. About ten years ago I drew him dipping his flock by the Walpole road. Electric fences are an inconspicuous and easily re-arranged way to keep the sheep in, or to move them from one pasture to another. Crossing the busy Walpole road with a large flock used to be difficult, but a tunnel was dug under it so that sheep could be moved from one side to the other without having to cross it. The current shepherd assembles energetic teams to shear them; they can get through many hundreds in a day and their quick, decisive and above all repetitive actions make good subjects.

Long before we came to the village, I'd made a lithograph of Heveningham Hall in an early group of architectural prints. George Ewart Evans had also once taken me to see an old horse-drawn wooden timber jim which at that time stood near the stables, a heavy and impressive piece of agricultural gear used for carting the heavy logs which the estate produced.

Ways

Suffolk's main roads are fast, well engineered and boring – they get one to and from London or the Midlands quickly, but while the passengers can enjoy the landscape, the driver has no time to take much in apart from the road signs, the other traffic and the weather. Old trees and cottages here and there still stand surprisingly close to the carriageway. The smaller roads are often very beautiful, fenced in by hedges instead of metal barriers, with many curves and corners and sometimes tunnelled through woodland or under natural archways of foliage. Trees often create an informal yet triumphal archway, sometimes made more dramatic by ivy, for the road to pass under; their trunks and branches can form a rigid square box, so definite and narrow that any more road-widening would entail felling a tree. Mechanical hedge-cutters create square openings simply by driving through the unruly new growth and small branches to make an aperture just big enough for a combine harvester to squeeze through. The minor lanes are still narrow enough to need passing places, though they are also being constantly if unofficially widened by heavy tractors and trailers. Their grass verges are not ideal places to walk on, but there are many footpaths, well-marked and maintained, where one can walk and enjoy a traffic-free view of the countryside.

When driving on the A12 or A14 one has just time to spot in passing prominent things like church towers and paired pylons from Sizewell, water towers festooned with mobile phone masts, rows of caravans for sale, shabby and run-down-looking farm buildings, old ivy-covered oaks, a tree-lined vista leading to a grand house, a thatched cottage barely a yard back from the roaring carriageway, and here and there the red bricks and curvy white bargeboards of the Victorian village schools. Where these roads by-pass a village or small town they siphon off some of its through traffic, but in the process they also eat up a swathe of countryside and inevitably alter the character of whatever place is being by-passed. The landscape the stopping train from Ipswich passes through is more idyllic – the farmland without the commerce. Away from the main roads, minor roads and lanes are narrower still, with varying amounts of grassy space or kerbs beside them or at their edges – sometimes barely enough to stand on. But the road to Cratfield (overleaf) is a lovely place to walk as it meanders along the valley that contains our stream.

Suffolk roads tend often to bend or even turn at right angles round the corners of properties that must have preferred not to be tinkered with. But between Peasenhall and Heveningham there is a long stretch that was originally a portion of a Roman road, and is still straight enough for one to see far along it, through the surrounding and enclosing trees as if through a telescope. Driving along it feels as if one is exploring a peepshow perspective or a toy theatre stage set where limitless distance is suggested as each succeeding aperture in the scenery gets smaller than the last. It's obviously safest to draw roadside scenes, straight or bendy, from the edge of the road. The curves of carriageway, verges and trees make good subjects anyway; the bendy lane into our village is admirable in this respect, the foliage growing round and seeming to caress the metalled roadway which in spring is made narrower still by banks of cow parsley.

The group of neglected but lovely farm buildings above is on the outskirts of Sibton and near the prettily named village of Peasenhall, which stands at the far end (from us) of our nearest bit of Roman road. The Low Road to Laxfield (below right) takes one through several magical woodland tunnels, passing on the way a handsome farmhouse overlooking the meadows by the real River Blyth, a deconsecrated church, and a field with a large mixed herd of cattle and llamas or alpacas, within earshot of a turkey farm. Some of the bigger fields nearer us, like the one on the right, are edged by headlands, the grassy strips left unsown at the edge of a crop. These provide beautiful views and spaces, not always way-marked as official footpaths, where dog walkers and horse riders seem tolerated. But many of our lanes still carry quite fast traffic and some have little room at either side to walk on. A few are narrower still, like the one behind our pub which climbs up a mini-ravine where one hopes not to meet a car.

Footpaths, even when signed and way-marked, are not always well-trodden and the route may be a bit indeterminate here and there. This gives a sense of freedom that adds to the pleasure of walking. But other paths are narrow and more clearly defined: the one on the far side of our stream is easy enough to follow even when pleasantly overgrown in summer, as it squeezes through the gap between the new plantation, a cornfield, the old oaks and the bramble thickets that edge the stream. I've occasionally seen owls here, and there are often green woodpeckers, which alert one with their urgent-sounding cries. People walk their children and their dogs; our grandchildren find blackberries and oddly-shaped stones. In winter they're muddy and you can see through the hedges; summer foliage makes these paths mysterious and secret.

The road we use most often is the one into our nearest small town. Halesworth is pretty, with many banks, some still functioning, in a pedestrianized main street called the Thoroughfare which, while straight in the middle, has a notably sinuous approach which the buildings curl round. Every last Sunday in August a lively antiques market takes over the Thoroughfare.

The Halesworth road passes through the village of Walpole at whose further end stands the remarkable Walpole Old Chapel. In the late seventeenth century the Suffolk Independents, Puritans who had been repressively excluded from the Anglican Church after the Restoration, had to meet secretly wherever they could. To begin with this was in a farmhouse which they then enlarged by adding a second gable. Its interior is entirely of wood, shaped and softened by time into a very beautiful structure. The pale colour of the wood blends with the creamy-tinted brick floor. Most of the box pews are still there, as is the pulpit on the north wall with its canopy hanging above it. A gallery surrounds the other three walls. The detailing of pews and pulpit is as economical and practical as Shaker furniture. The roof is supported centrally by a strong and elegant wooden column looking very much like the ship's mast it probably once was. The main timbers of roof and galleries have settled into gentle curves which suggest age but not frailty. The overall impression this building makes is of thoughtful people who came here to listen to each other's words and thoughts rather than to perform a preordained ritual and say things they didn't believe.

Sowing

Unsurprisingly, most of what surrounds us in Suffolk are fields. This might sound like a recipe for monotony, and sometimes it is. But their appearance is constantly changing, under varying weather, skies, light, and different crops and seasons. The crops immediately around us are mainly wheat, rape and barley; others have included green peas and broad beans. Potatoes, onions, kale and cauliflower are grown on the light sandier soil nearer the coast.

In the early months of the year, winter has by now really set in and dug in its heels. The countryside looks dead, left over, a black and brown anti-climax. The snow when it comes looks pretty, traditional and harmless from the main roads, but turns tricky on the narrow minor ones; after the thaw, remnants of it cling on in shaded furrows and ditches and in heaps by the roadsides until we're tired of it. The overall bareness is revealing. As last year's growth in hedges and ditches dies, turns white and rattles in the wind, all the secrets of fields, woods and gardens are exposed. When it's cold and dry you can walk on the hard soil without sinking into mud. In the furrows and tractor tracks, puddles gleam or flash as they reflect the thin low sunlight. You can see the structures of bare trees and where last autumn's stubble hasn't been ploughed in you can see every stalk.

In January and February, hedges and thickets are still black and the surviving plant stalks around them have been bleached white. The other colours are the browns and greens of the fields, which only begin to sparkle when the sun comes out and the coloured fields are lighter in tone than the sky. The landscape seems asleep; through the leafless hedges you can see whatever is beyond, see the birds in the bare branches of the trees. You notice the remains of last year's stubble overlaid at a slightly different angle by this year's new sowing; last year's dried grass and undergrowth lie at the edges of hedgerows and under the rows of newly planted saplings. Some fields are still being ploughed. A tractor is raking over rape fields which still look thin and unpromising. They are thick with pigeons despite the tethered plastic eagles, the alarming bangs of the bird-scarers, and the empty fertiliser bags like ghostly scarecrows fluttering in the wind. Hares race about paying no attention to these. In March and April, blackthorn and catkins enliven the hedgerows and you sense, or hope, that spring is on the way.

I first drew this view on a sunny morning but with a cold wind. The field had two rows or directions of planting – last year's wheat stubble, and this year's rape criss-crossing it at a slightly different angle. There were the sounds of larks, blackbirds, a distant chiff-chaff, woodpeckers, the fierce song of a wren in the hedge, doves cooing and the intermittent bangs of bird scarers. By 8.30 the sky was clear and the morning warmed up surprisingly. In the hedgerow by the stream the blackthorn was blossoming but not quite full out yet. A few people were about, walking their dogs; I could also hear riders on the far side of the stream, and out of sight in the field beyond them a heavy tractor was pulling something that breaks the ground lightly but doesn't turn it over as a plough would. Or it might just have been spraying or fertilising the young crop. In the early spring you can still see into secret places like the field ponds that later become hidden behind undergrowth. The fields dry out and the hedgerows turn green.

Dark skies make the fields beneath them luminous and dramatic. When the crop is oilseed rape it quickly turns in spring from a just-discernible sprinkling of florets into a yellow blaze that hides the tousled-looking greenery beneath. Just across the road from our house is our neighbour's white wooden bungalow, in summer quite invisible even from the field but in the winter easily seen through the bare trees. It had been built after the war for the district nurse. When we arrived it was lived in by two elderly sisters, not very outgoing at first but quite friendly later on. They bought fish for their several cats from the van which used to come every week, so the bungalow always smelt a bit fishy. Their own garden was overgrown but when we were away and it was warm enough they would come across the road and sit in ours. Another early neighbour at the far end of the terrace had been a keen gardener and though friendly enough across his garden gate was inclined to be crotchety and a bit critical of newcomers.

The rape crop is in full flower in early May, looking at its best against heavy skies. When I first drew these the hedgerow on the left was still unbroken. Now there is an opening halfway up it to let the combine through instead of having to negotiate the difficult and muddy opening onto the road. The distance between the tractors' tramlines is determined by the length of the crop-sprayer's arms.

When drawing outside you notice birdsong. The chiffchaffs have come by mid-April, their repetitive and monotonous song still an evocative part of spring and summer and warmer days. At this time of year you can see them flitting about high up in the bare trees, but when the leaves come fully out they're almost invisible, though still audible. Every spring there used also to be a pair of willow wrens in this same hedgerow. They look exactly like chiffchaffs but have a quite different song, lovely and subtle and touching. But for the last few years I've not heard them here. They build a hollow spherical nest down near ground level. I once found one of them when biking by the edge of the A12.

Last year the spring had been late and cold, and even by June there had not been many warm days. By mid-May the hawthorn blossom was thinning and disappearing, and most of the rape flowers had blown away, leaving yellow only the backward parts of the field that a month earlier had looked sickly and unlikely ever to grow at all, but which were now still in full bloom. After a mostly warm and sunny day, the sky darkened and thundered, and heavy rain pelted down for twenty minutes flattening the big daisies in the front garden, yet after a few hours they perked up again and faced up to the sky once more. Really dark skies mean imminent rain which besides soaking one makes watercolours run. These three pictures were all made within two minutes' walk from the house so I got back dryshod. It's frustrating to have to stop work, but skies like these make good subjects – they show up the tones and colour of whatever is beneath them and the showers are often followed by clear skies and renewed energy.

One sunny morning beneath a completely blue sky it's warmer out in the sun than in the house. Through the window we see a pair of hares running madly about in the rape field, and lots of birds – even a woodpecker – at the feeder in the crab apple tree. Everything outside is bursting into leaf – trees, garden plants, a thin mist of whiteness where blackthorn blossoms in the hedges. In the causeway you can hardly see the sky any more for the foliage; elsewhere, oaks and many trees are still bare, but ashes are just beginning to mist over; chestnuts are full out but have no candles yet; the trees with catkins are fully out. The sounds are of the shepherd's dogs barking in the distance, some light planes and a helicopter. Then greenery reappears; celandines and snowdrops, daffodils and primroses turn up in the still-frosty grass and the brown remnants shrivel in last year's flowerbeds. The trees begin to turn green, the oaks usually last of all.

The field at the back of the house and just beyond the stream is low-lying and parts of it are quite wet, which means that in early summer it's lush and beautiful. There's a small pond at the end of the line of dark trees on the right. The trees on the left are growing by a path, an extension of the causeway and a good place to walk. In the middle of this field there used to be an old oak with a hollow trunk in which our children liked to play (overleaf). But quite early on in our time there, when the field was under wheat, the tree got in the way of the combines and was felled. I often drew this view up the valley; these are fairly early pictures. The low damp part of this field is now a plantation of oak and beech, the ash saplings having died.

Later in June, after a hot week of blue skies, time seems to stand still. The sun has suddenly stopped shining; the trees are darkening, and the corn is turning a warmer shade of green.

These three groups of trees, which stand within 200 yards of each
other, are very different in density of foliage and in outline. Those
above are mostly oaks, solid and heavy with their projecting wooden
antlers visible; there is also a hawthorn and an elder in the middle.
This corner where three big fields meet is unusually beautiful, due
partly to the wide grassy headlands at the edge of the crops, and
also to the offer of two alternative routes into the distance. These
routes are emphasised by the light tracks pressed into the grass by
tractors and Land-Rovers. The shadows falling across the grass
emphasise the shapes of the ground and the crops.

The three tall trees in the second sketch are poplars. There are
many groups or clusters of them on the distant skylines around
the village, sticking well up above the hedges and smaller trees,
but often looking a bit dog-eared or half blown away. The big willow
on the right is lighter and more transparent than the oaks, and its
edges more feathery; you can see into the dark branches within
the foliage more easily than you can into an oak's.

Hay is the first crop to be harvested and is either left to dry in the sun or baled straight away. Our stream, having run through the village, here passes between the two fields nearest to the parkland of Heveningham Hall. The two upper drawings were made there one midsummer morning – luckily, as it turned out, for later that day the bales had all been carted away. The pretty farmhouse in the distance used to be the home farm on the estate, the one providing for its own needs. Like the small thatched cottage at this end of the village, it can be seen from the hall as a picturesque element in an ingeniously planned and maintained landscape. The stream here is shaded by an idyllic-looking group of willows with rushes beneath them.

There are more willows by the stream where it passes Huntingfield Hall, and where the hay bales (opposite) are stacked at the edge of the public footpath. This footpath leads up the slope to the Queen's Oak and on across the high ground with fine distant views over the fields and patches of woodland near Cookley.

At the far side of a nearby field a small ditch (p.65), now richly overgrown, lies between two sloping fields of rape. At the top of the field on the left is another field pond, almost hidden in midsummer by the rushes, grasses and flowers that surround it. As I quietly approach I can hear in it a moorhen with a chick, but when I get there they have hidden away among the rushes. In a tree a few yards away is a small bird, quite noisy, that must be a whitethroat. The first time I remember seeing or noticing a field pond was when floating over it in a balloon – a dark circle in the corner of a field of corn, with no apparent purpose. Beyond the pond one can see in the distance the Cookley road, itself almost hidden between steep banks, and the newly-mown hayfields, their lines of hay following the gentle curves and irregularities of the field and adding their own. When the sun is high they are hard to see but in the low evening sun light these rows of hay cast shadows which briefly make their curving lines a striking element in the landscape.

On our two nearest fields the corn is beginning to change colour, from bright sharp green towards tawny or olive. The tramlines are deepening and their junctions now more precise and more complicated. As July approaches, the wheat will gradually turn yellow and then darken and its upright ears start to droop, growing first browner and then greyer as the sun dries and bleaches them. The two fields in these pictures share an opening onto the lane by our house. The picture (below right) shows it a few weeks before harvesting. I've often drawn this opening and the trees on either side of it and from different angles – usually peacefully rural but at harvest time busy with combines and the tractors taking the laden grain trailers back to the nearby farm. Almost immediately afterwards come ploughs, scarifiers, harrows and rollers, all now able to spread out wide as they as they till the field or to fold up narrow for the road.

If you look for them, Suffolk abounds in fascinating things – left-over relics, often alluring like the primitive-looking oddities of traction engines and the beautiful and subtle curves of old wooden carts, now preserved and cherished for the craftsmanship and ingenuity amounting to artistry that went into them. There are many examples of these – barns, ploughs, carts, a maltings pay-shed, along with good historic photos of the people who used them – in the Museum of East Anglian Life at Stowmarket. Other less hallowed remains have survived simply because they are durable or indestructible. There is a wartime Nissen-hut on the edge of our village which has become increasingly skeletal as its corrugated iron cladding rusts away to nothing, each year leaving more open spaces for the dense plants inside to push up through. It is now impenetrable.

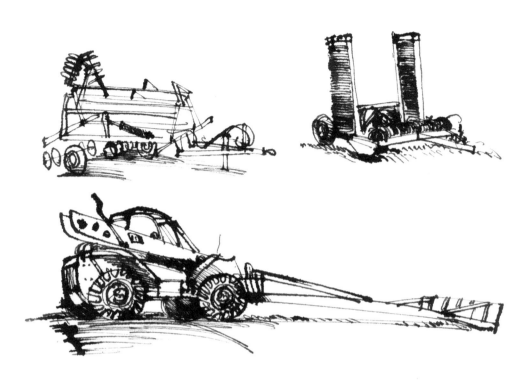

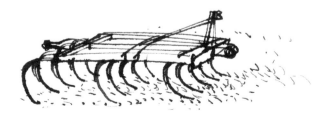

Bits of heavy metal farm machinery often remain for years tucked away and overgrown in out-of-the-way corners of fields, probably because they might still come in handy or have been forgotten or are too much trouble to move away, until one day you notice that they have suddenly and inexplicably vanished. Their dereliction is part of their charm. In the seemingly disused, weedy and undesirable corner patch of a field beyond the church, this tall Wellingtonia, the church tower, the digger and the slowly disintegrating plastic silo all make good silhouettes against the sky. Nearby are fragments of old breeze block walls sheltering rotting bales of straw. Such left-over corners made good places for our children to play in and hide. In summer they are full of baby rabbits – I once saw a buzzard flapping heavily away from here with one in its beak. Here I could draw undisturbed, enjoy the changing light and the wild plants flourishing. Now it's gone I even miss the yellow digger.

Nature

The oak is the most familiar and characteristic Suffolk tree. Its whole appearance suggests sturdiness. It can be seen everywhere – standing solitary in fields, in hedgerows, occasionally in groups; splendid and majestic in parkland. There are plenty of them around the village – many among the myriads of recently planted saplings; young trees like ours in the garden; fine mature specimens; others now elderly and often ivy-covered and antlered by bare dead branches projecting beyond the shrinking leafy core; aged and decrepit veterans, nourished only by the sap still rising through pathetic remnants of bark.

Oaks have been much painted. They appear in many of Constable's best-known works; 'Old' Crome's painting of the Poringland Oak in Tate Britain captures accurately the tree's structure inside its bobbly-edged foliage. And oaks have acquired both practical and symbolic aspects. The heavy structural timbers and wide floorboards in our house are of oak; our children and grandchildren have climbed up, played on and hidden in the hollow oaks nearby, like the one opposite. Oaks have become vivid symbols of beauty, strength, endurance, and eventual frailty – as indeed of our country's dwindling international significance, which like an old oak itself clings on only in a much depleted form.

The landscape around the village is being transformed by the intensive planting of young saplings, mostly oak, beech and (until recently) ash, which had to be expensively culled when they became infected with ash dieback. I like drawing the recently planted young trees, the amazing regularity of the rows, their patterns and shadows, the grasses at their base and the marks of the tractors between them; the mechanical precision of the planting process itself, and the symmetrical perspectives of the straight rows as they follow the curves of the sloping land they stand on.

The oak above has hung on for a long time. I was intrigued by the intricacies of its branches, especially when the bare tree is stark against the sky. Its slowly disintegrating silhouette reminded me of the lacy coral outcrops I once saw sticking up out of the sea from the reef around a Pacific island. The coral's eerie shapes in the dusk were in the past thought by the islanders to embody the spirits of their ancestors, an idea that despite its glowering black eye this battered tree would never have suggested to me.

A few years ago I drew another old oak (opposite) standing by the stream behind the old rectory. Most of its bark on this side has since fallen off or been pulled away from the main trunk, yet the fragment that remains on the other side is still able to keep the remnants of its branches alive and their leaves nourished.

The effects of ivy growing on a big tree are easily overlooked in summer when the darker greenery of the ivy disappears within the tree's own foliage. But it can sometimes look very pretty, giving the bare tree the semblance of greenery and life even in mid-winter, while in reality the ivy is slowly throttling it. The tree on the left stood by the stream behind the old rectory, its trunk half-hidden beneath the complex tangle of thick ivy limbs. I was struck by their oddity and complexity, gradually choking and sucking the life from the big tree and looking like intricate plumbing.

The pattern of an oak's deeply furrowed bark made me think of the chunky texture of a ploughed field, its different parts separating from and rejoining each other with tantalising complexity, as if in a swaying dance. I made the study of the tree above about eight years ago, before most of its bark on this side at least had peeled away. The drawing took two mornings and since the whole surface was fascinating but repetitive I had to stick markers on it to form a sort of boundary or target area to remind me what my drawing was centred on. From time to time I'd notice insects patiently climbing up in the crevices.

As oaks age they look gradually more fragile, bent and generally done-for, yet even far into their decline they survive and also become increasingly interesting to draw. I'm intrigued by the intricacies of their few remaining branches, especially when the bare wintry tree is silhouetted against the sky. The two drawings of the same tree in winter and summer (top left and opposite) show its contasting shape and general appearance with and without leaves; prettier perhaps in summer but easier to understand in winter.

Our nearest handsome, sizeable and mature oak (overleaf) stands just across the Cookley road at the corner of a long meadow edged by the stream, which here is very narrow but still pretty. The meadow is a level stretch between the gently sloping fields that continue to flank it all the way up the valley as far as the next village. This tree is a fascinating specimen, which has thinned out sufficiently to let one see into its central branch structure. There is plenty of life left in it – its own, plus all the owls, woodpeckers, pigeons, magpies, jays, crows, tree creepers, wrens, thrushes and chiffchaffs and myriad insects that make use of it.

The elder is one of the later trees to blossom, its amazing display of round clumps of flowers hanging heavily over its quite fragile structure. The blackthorn is the first hedgerow tree to blossom and to enliven the still wintry-looking hedges with its promise of spring. But the blossom I find most intensely beautiful is the hawthorn's (overleaf) with its dazzling strings of white flowers cascading like foam over its dark interior and tumbling down to meet the Queen Anne's Lace rising from the grasses beneath it.

Wild plants are the bit of the landscape closest to us – nearer to our eyes than the ground we stand on. We brush against them, touch them, feel them. They can be hard or prickly or stinging, or soft and cushiony like mosses; useful or beautiful, like the lovely flowering grasses that give me hay fever.

Plants make good visual screens, decorative, defensive or protective. Climbing ones like hops can disguise eyesores or decorate and enhance stark uprights like old trees or electricity poles just by climbing up them. In spring, cow parsley or Queen Anne's Lace can both enhance the shape of a roadway and at corners and crossroads conceal approaching traffic. I like drawing cow parsley for its structure and height, and its saucer-like blossom. It's followed in July by hogweed, which looks good at the edge of a cornfield or even when accidentally left standing in the middle of it. When growing out of long grass in a shady place by the stream, hogweed plants form a jungle, warm and steamy; they also have fine silhouettes at dusk as the light fades. In summer, plants almost completely conceal streams and ditches, making it easier to stumble into them. By autumn, the tall plants have died leaving their skeletons standing as russet and brown reminders among the surrounding grass-greens and yellows.

Alexanders are widespread early in spring but more striking later on when they flower, both in the fields or if they accidentally arrive in the garden. Their flowers form rounder, more globular shapes than the flatter plate-like flowers of cow parsley and hogweed.

I've always liked dock leaves, for soothing nettle stings when I was a boy and later for drawing, because their big leaves look temptingly simple to draw, but, in fact, aren't. They still look lovely even when they eventually turn brown, damp and lacy.

The hogweed flower in the pencil sketch below was as snugly enfolded inside its pod as a foetus in the womb, a thought which came to me as I drew it. The process of bursting out was over surprisingly quickly, perhaps within half an hour. It was a warm still morning in the low field beyond the stream, and the other splendid hogweed flowers were already fully spread out like umbrellas. I've often drawn them and always liked them even when they were getting a bit past their best and were covered with insects. They go on looking good as dried-out skeletons.

Hovering unpredictably over the Suffolk landscape is the very useful sky. These landscapes are too horizontal to be as spectacular as those of hillier counties: the distance and most of the drama is overhead, as it is in old Flemish paintings. Since the sky is often cloudy, the distant views you seldom get here across the landscape itself are supplied instead by the skyscapes. These can be perspectives of the bases of solid, mountainous cumulus or successive layers of flatter, higher ones, or mere cotton-wool tufts against a clear summer blue.

Skies can also be delightful and inspiring or sullen and foreboding. They can cheerfully promise to be about to clear or tantalisingly refuse to do so, thinning to allow only small glints of sunlight through and then stubbornly drawing their curtain back over them again. These gaps between clouds serve as spotlights on the landscapes below; the early English watercolourists used these skilfully to dramatise features or patches of interest in dull or flat-toned scenes. Watching cloud shadows moving across fields and revealing their dips and hummocks is one of the pleasures of drawing or painting in the open.

Grey skies with breaks in them are beautiful when you can see through to pale blue sky and distant mountains of sunlit cloud. An evening sky that had seemed to have settled into greyness can end with a sudden low burst of sun down near the horizon. Everyone must have enjoyed the transition from the chilly greyness of dawn to the first gleaming fragment of the sun, or in the evening the spectacle of a blazing red sunset sky seeping away to paler, pink-tinted clouds and soon to darkness. Clouds sometimes reflect the colour of the landscape beneath them – their greys a little greenish at midsummer, and later slightly tinted with yellow at harvest time.

Reaping

After the rape's spring flowering, the cereal crops' ripening provides the year's next big colour change and transformation; even the long swathes of cloud disappearing into the distance maybe five miles away faintly tinged by the yellow crops beneath. This is a good time of year to draw outside, with warm days, long evenings and school holidays so that we can spend more time in the country.

As a schoolboy at the end of the war I'd spent several Augusts on a friend's farm, gathering the sheaves of prickly barley, thistly oats and heavy wheat, and stooking or stacking them upright in pairs, about five sheaves to each side, to dry; and eventually tossing them up with pitchforks onto a cart. So I found out early on what an exhausting and long-drawn-out process getting the harvest in was in those days. Nowadays combines can do it almost instantly, leaving behind them a striking landscape of bales of straw like small neat monoliths, oblong or cylindrical, sometimes wrapped in plastic, to be built later into solid stacks or high walls – all of these tempting to draw. Ploughing often follows almost immediately, creating unseasonably brown fields again in summer. Sometimes conventional deep ploughing is replaced by more lightly scarifying the field surface, but the solidly impacted tracks of the tramlines may need to be broken up first.

Sometimes a subject is something I've already seen, perhaps many times, and held in my mind to return to later. On other occasions, it may be something that suddenly looks or seems so interesting that I want to get it down on paper straight away without caring much whether it's done carefully or sketchily. Here the subjects are the varying colours of three landscapes – the different hues of trees and crops, the darkness of a sky interesting not only for its threatening character but also for the way it changes the apparent colours and tones of the fields beneath or even of a neutral and near monochromatic scene. Although these three are all of the same nearby field, they began differently and under very contrasting skies. In the already half-cut corner of the field (below left) I painted straight off and quickly with no preliminary drawing. The dark-sky scene above took two or three sittings, though only on the first day was the sky so dramatic.

These subjects reflect the changing phases and skies in a day or two just before getting the crop in. Variables like the nature of the sky, the light and the position of the sun make clearer the subtleties in the lie of the land. In these ever more intensely mechanised landscapes I grew interested in the sometimes quite intricate patterns made in the crops by the tractor tracks, patterns that have now become as characteristic of the present-day farming landscape as the fields themselves. A more timeless aspect of harvest time is the sharp edge of the standing crop (overleaf), left as the combine crosses to and fro or round and round it, just as it had been in the past by human reapers. This uncut edge has interested many artists in the past, from the early Italians and Breughel on. John Nash in the 1950s made a lithograph (p.32/3) of a similar and supposedly unchangeable harvest scene, then still full of the people – farmworkers, youths and girls, onlookers – now vanished from the harvest fields.

The road to Cookley has several smallish hills with shallow dips between them. The scene above is one of these, with yet another unnamed Blyth tributary trickling along out of sight under the trees on the left, seen in the morning after the first few circuits of the combine harvester the evening before. There is a well-signposted path or right-of-way along the length of several fields here with a few wooden footbridges, but no one was walking on it. Cookley church is in the distance. The perspectives of crop, trees, distant hedges, stubble and sky make it a stunning stretch of landscape.

On the right are two current examples of the classic harvest subject, the neat and precise edge of the half-cut crop and the suddenly-revealed stubble after the reapers (now the combine) have passed. The almost black horizon line of trees and hedgerows separating the bleached cornfield from the sky is another characteristic Suffolk feature. In each one can see the swirling lines of the curving skyline, the edge of standing corn, the lines of straw and chaff, the stubble, the bits of straw left uncut (or unsown), and the close-toned yellowy browns of harvest fields against a grey sky.

The paleness of the ripening fields make the surrounding hedges
and trees look almost black. The clean-cut edge of standing corn
allows one a glimpse of its mysterious, hidden interior in which
butterflies, insects, hares, pheasants and partridges have until now
sheltered, unseen and secure. The harvesting is now done by the
combine driver and the pair of tractor drivers who take it in turns
to cart away the newly harvested grain in brimming open trucks.
A fourth man, probably the farmer himself, may drive up to check
on how things are going. But except when they leave their vehicles
for a break or to stretch their legs and have a chat, these people
are almost invisible. The combine drivers in particular are also
very busy – not just with steering the machine straight and backing
into awkward corners but also checking on their instruments the
weight and moisture content of the crop they're cutting,
information that is also being sent meanwhile to the contractors'

headquarters. Harvesting has to go on round the clock before a break in the weather delays it. When it is at its height we hear the constant sound of combine harvesters up to two miles away, the tractors pulling heavy trailer-loads of corn rumbling down the lane past our house, and the hum of the grain drier in the big farm. To an onlooker it all now seems to be over very quickly – enormous fields polished off in an afternoon or if need be finished overnight. The uncut areas grow smaller and smaller until they are reduced to narrow strips or triangles. Occasionally hares escape from these refuges at the last minute and race across the stubble to safety in a hedge or over the horizon; fewer people now seem inclined to hang around hoping to shoot them. The field of stubble (above) on the Cookley-Halesworth road, had just been cut, the combine had finished its work, leaving tracks full of chaff. The field overleaf was drawn with a ruling-pen in watercolour instead of ink.

The combine above was breasting the hill behind our house as it emptied the grain into the trailer. I like watching this process as the two vehicles keep pace with each other, like aircraft refuelling in mid-air. After the field has been cut there is a sense of peace but also anti-climax, present last year in the scene on the opposite hilltop. From here the Hall is still visible in the distance although from the road alongside it is already screened by new tree planting.

Until about thirty years ago, the straw and chaff remaining after the harvest used to be left lying on the stubble and was often routinely burnt off. This was a spectacular process, especially towards dusk, with the whole field seeming to be aflame and columns of smoke drifted across the roads or rising high into the sky where you could see them from far away. This burning got rid of the harvest's left-overs but was hard on the wildlife in the fields.

Bales come in various shapes – cylinders like Swiss rolls or the sections of toppled Greek marble columns that lie where they fell in Sicilian temple sites, or plain rectangular blocks that have the same appeal and sense of endless possibilities that children's building bricks have. They can be held together by string or plastic netting or packaged in green or black shiny waterproof sheeting. The bales may be left lying for a bit wherever they fell out of the combine, and then fork-lifted onto trucks and carted away into a barn or built into a stack. Sometimes they are stacked in immense blocks like a fortress. On pig farms they serve as barriers or windbreaks or tall walls, and I suppose end up as bedding. They may just be left to eventually disintegrate. At dusk the oblong ones resemble standing stones like those at Stonehenge and have something of the same monumental quality. When the cylindrical ones are made of pea straw instead of wheat they look soft and a bit floppy and sag like cushions. All are interesting to draw and their effect on the summer landscape has been striking. When scattered across an enormous field these straw monoliths look splendid.

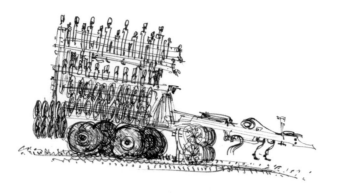

As farms get larger, mechanisation intensifies: the tractors all getting bigger and more comfortable, some with tracks replacing wheels; combine harvesters that take off and fold back their cutting arms so that they can be towed through a gate or along a narrow lane. The harrow above ingeniously unfolds itself like one of those toys that transform themselves from people or monsters into vehicles. I had a ride on a combine once; half an hour sailing high over a crop of flax was a good experience. I'm amazed by the skill and patience of the seemingly tireless drivers, tacking to and fro across their sea of corn in the field opposite our garden at night with their headlamps blazing.

Compared with the relatively simple and basic vintage farm machines that turn up at rallies and steam fairs, the current ones look phenomenally expensive, always getting heavier, cleverer and more powerful – the combines wider and most of them painted in bright primary colours. All these have great fascination and add to the interest of the fields; but they also make one wonder about their cost to the farmer and the effect of all this elaborate and heavy gear weighing down on the structure of the soil. Others though are still small and simple, like the old-style baler that needs a tractor to pull it and excretes the bales of straw from its back end like an animal, or more sinister, like the crop-sprayer appearing over the brow of a hill with its poison arms spread menacingly like outstretched wings.

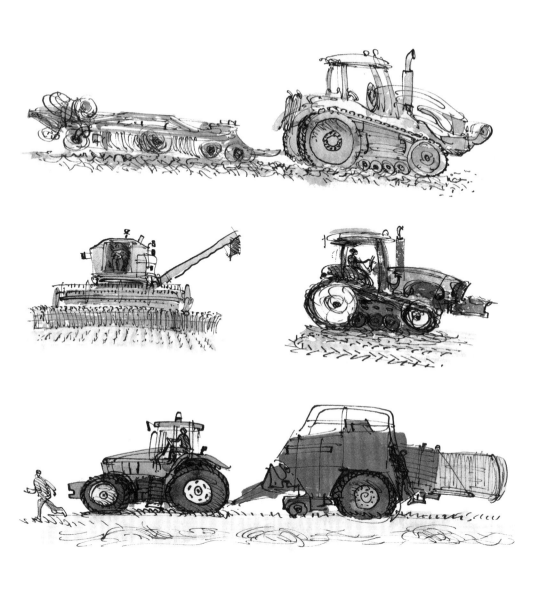

After the hectic blitzkrieg of getting in the harvest and the ploughing, harrowing, rolling, and sowing that follow, the fields calm down. In the pre-mechanised past, Suffolk farm workers then routinely left home, going off by train to seasonal work in the brewers' maltings at Burton to turn the barley they had just harvested into malt. The fields are emptier of people anyway now, so the contrast with the past is less obvious.

Autumn is still a time for maintenance, hedging, tidying up. The days shorten but it stays warm; blackberries and sloes appear in the hedges; the tall weeds die and bleach to white. The trees begin to change colour and the leaves start to fall, but not all at once – oaks, late to turn green in spring, stay green longest. Fields of crows feed on the stubble and flocks of sunlit seagulls follow the plough behind the tractor. The patterns these tramlines make, their curvy junctions and crossing points, are still almost everywhere. They become so well established and hardened by late summer (see p.224) that they need to be broken up before a field can be ploughed.

As one approaches the plateau of High Suffolk to the west of our village the character of the landscape changes slightly; one notices successive lines of hedgerows instead of just one, and the dips between the slopes where the streams run. In late summer the countryside is quieter again. As the stubble fields are ploughed the landscape loses its straw-coloured uniformity and returns to cooler and more varied hues.

The field pond is now almost hidden by the rushes, and the tall grasses and flowers that surround it. Ponds in open countryside are easily overlooked – tucked away from roads and hidden in their own depressions. They were once important as fishponds and as reserves of water for livestock. They are also now thought important for helping to hold back field water that would otherwise drain too quickly into lower fields and flood plains. Even in this driest part of Britain prolonged rainy spells can make big puddles well up in low lying fields and temporarily turn them into lakes which for a day or two look surprising and enchanting.

Estuaries

In Suffolk you don't often see estuaries until you're almost upon them – seldom are you on ground high enough to afford unexpected glimpses of them, light or sparkling in the distance. From the splendid Orwell Bridge at Ipswich you can't see the water even when you're driving across it. Where the rivers widen out into estuaries, as at Blythburgh and Snape and on the Deben near Woodbridge (opposite), embankments (often protected by posts or stakes) were in the past built up on either side of the channel to keep the tidal water from flooding over into the marshes. Though you now have to be wary of new gaps in them, these embankments offer excellent estuary views over wide expanses of tidal water or mud, often edged by long stretches of sedge. Gaunt oak tree skeletons still stand maybe a hundred yards out in the tidal mud on what had once been dry land. At the current water's edge are brambles, oaks, and stretches of muddy or sandy beach, often with a boat or two floating or lying beached. The Alde near Iken is such a place, wild and lonely, with only the sounds of reed birds invisible in the sedge, marsh harriers in the sky and shelduck, herons, gulls and terns on the mud. You can sometimes see egrets, curlews, avocets and even a spoonbill there too, and maybe an old Thames barge apparently sailing through the distant fields.

Tide mills harness the power of water from a reservoir filled at high tide and then allowed as the tide goes down to flow back into the estuary through the mill's water-wheel. I first drew the tide mill at Woodbridge when making an early lithograph in the l960s. Its timbers were then still clad in reddish-brown corrugated iron sheets, an intriguing material to draw because of its strong linear pattern. (Corrugated cardboard stops my pencils and brushes rolling about on the studio desk.) But soon afterwards the mill was restored and its surfaces weather-boarded and painted white.

Mills have simple and comprehensible shapes which reflect their practicality. It's also fun to explore them and work out the ingenious mechanisms by which their cog-wheels transfer the directional power of wind or falling water into the rotary power that turned the mill-wheels that ground the corn. This mill's all-timber interior reminded me of the Walpole chapel (p.136). From its windows you look out over the water and mud of the Deben estuary. Mud has a surprising ability to reflect; however much the wind ripples and darkens the surface of an estuary's open water, the mud at its edges goes on gleaming and reflecting sky and sun.

Maltings were built where grain (most commonly barley, for making beer and malt extract) was abundant and could be turned into malt and where transport by rail or water existed to bring the grain and take the malt away. The traditional process of making it is quite complicated: grains of barley were first soaked in water to make them germinate, then spread out on the heated malt house or maltings floor to dry them in order to halt the germination, and then roasted or kiln-dried. This drying process was used until the l940s, when kiln-drying began to be abandoned in favour of bigger industrial fans blowing the hot air.

The maltings at Snape owed their existence to two natural features – the rich farming country nearby and the navigable estuary to bring in the barley and then ship the malt away. Most maltings are far less spectacular than at Snape or Mistley, but many remain monumental even when abandoned or converted into flats – industrial structures that besides looking splendid have also become a characteristic part of the countryside. Their bold plain shapes made them good simple subjects for my early lithographs.

In the wide and low-lying landscape of the Blyth flood plain, just before it widens into a full estuary, Blythburgh's church – often called the Cathedral of the Marshes – is the dominant feature, a beautiful distant landmark from the fields below. Inside, it is light, airy and bare. Among the various wooden bench ends, some of them a bit dull, the headless figure of a harvester with a sickle grasping a wheatsheaf is noteworthy: touchingly well-observed, as if by a craftsman who had closely observed his subject. Its realism makes a good foil to the idealised formality of the lovely wooden angels, graceful and perfect, pinned to the tie-beams above. The angels are arranged in pairs, facing in opposite directions but joined at the waist by a decorative roof-boss. During the Cold War other fliers, American A-10 Warthogs, also usually in pairs, constantly and noisily overflew the Blyth, Alde and Deben estuaries on the way to and from their airbase at Bentwaters, now happily abandoned. Its name, originally taken from a local farm, aptly reflects these meandering estuaries. The drawing of it includes the remote Wantisden church near the end of the runway.

Estuary shores are an acquired but rewarding taste, their essential elements being space, distance, wildness and inaccessibility. In the marshes that often edge them one has to watch out for sudden unexpectedly deep inlets, reedbeds and a feeling of being lost. Here and there one may glimpse a farmhouse or farm buildings, isolated and far from a public road but with a splendid view of the wide stretch of water or mud, which shimmers or glitters in front of it according to the tide. From a field near Iken where cars can park you can often see the distant sail of the Thames barge based at Snape winding its way along the tortuous channel called Troublesome Reach. From the shore the boat seems puzzlingly to be turning back and forth on itself before it reaches the wider and deeper water. If you walk out on the embankment you pass skeletal boats half-sunk in the mud and see the distant Snape concert hall. There are maltings also in the watercolour overleaf of an Ipswich quayside made in 1955 when this inner dock, now full of fibreglass launches, was still part of an industrial port.

Coast

The sea is a restless and tantalising subject. Clouds and sunlight, tide and waves and season transform it from foreboding gloom to sparkling playfulness. Some of its moods are menacing and awe-inspiring; others are more intelligible and repetitive enough to let one work out how waves form, build up, fold or tumble over and break down into foam. Paul Nash painted this process vividly. These constantly changing effects are timeless – they have been going on forever. But on a shorter timescale, people have always been altering the appearance of this coast as ports have appeared, flourished, silted up and vanished, just as others have erected their buildings on convenient cliffs only to see them crumble into the sea. More recent attempts to safeguard this coast against high tides erosion and longshore drift have begun, failed and been abandoned. The fishing industry has gradually diminished, leaving in Suffolk mainly evocative relics. Its buildings and gear make coastal places look by turns run-down or fascinating, done-for or sparky. There are still plenty of boats, a few older wooden ones that remain afloat, and relics of others that lurk rotting and half-submerged in the mud. But in general fishing, hereabouts at least, has now been replaced by tourism and its one-time towns and villages have been adopted by the retired.

Covehithe is on few signposts. Its spectacular ruined church almost conceals a newer and smaller chapel which is still in use. The ruins have been well conserved; they are surrounded by a churchyard in which at midsummer the gravestones are almost invisible beneath the beautiful flowering grasses, feathery and enchanting and greyer in colour than the greenery beneath.

From here a twenty minute walk took me to a long empty stretch of sandy beach, stretching away to the north under a low cliff which is not so dramatically high as at Dunwich (p.252) but seems to be crumbling gently away even so. On the fields leading up towards the cliff edge was a windswept crop of barley, already paler in colour than the green cornfields elsewhere; the low trees by the path had been blown almost flat by the North Sea wind. Between the beach and the farmland were sedge-fringed lagoons, now a nature reserve, over which a flock of geese were honking and circling before eventually flying off in V-formation. Some tree-stumps and roots were lying about on the beach, half-buried in the sand and neatly trimmed but still looking both ornamental and surreal. The place was tranquil and empty; the only intrusive element was the distant pig farm beyond the lagoons.

Stanley Spencer painted Southwold's beach from further along the road to the left, looking down on 1930s families sheltering on the shingle in the lee of the wooden groynes, their coloured windbreaks hung with damp towels. Two generations before Spencer, Wilson Steer had drawn more romantically windswept women and children on the beach here; facing the sea, the scene still looks essentially the same. The beach road ends now in a line of small boats and marine gear where the Blyth estuary reaches the sea. A small ferry boat takes you across the Blyth to pretty Walberswick (above, twenty years ago); both sides of the river now look more prosperous and a bit more commercial.

From Walberswick you can walk south along the beach or slightly
inland, a lovely route through woodland and then down to sedge
and shingle, passing the stark remains of a wind pump once used
for draining the reed beds. The reeds are cut in April and stacked
beside the track in bundles ready to be carted away on trailers. The
marsh is crossed by narrow ditches and pools with ducks, swans,
waders and an egret on them. Once you reach the shingle beach
with breaking waves curling up its steep slope you can see your
distant goal, the line of houses and pub of Dunwich. As you walk
along the shifting shingle or at low tide on the narrow strip of damp
sand, they seem for a while to get no nearer until at last you forget
them, notice other things, and suddenly you're there.

Dunwich is our nearest bit of beach and stretch of coast and consequently the one we know the best. We used to see fishing boats coming in here from the sea, sometimes several at a time, and what often looked like big catches of cod being landed. The boats were then pulled up the shingle to its crest by winches housed in black-tarred boxes at the top, and finally rotated on a greasy turntable to face the sea again. Now the fishing has dwindled and barely survives, with only one or two boats still working – far fewer than the number of winch sheds laid out in a line at the top of the beach. This overlooks the low ground, now a kind of sedgy lagoon, behind the ridge of shingle. In medieval times this ridge stretched to Southwold, and the Blyth estuary had to flow down behind it as far as Dunwich before it could reach the sea. The estuary here had

been in medieval times a substantial dockyard and port. But in the fourteenth century it silted up, the port declined, the Blyth broke through the shingle ridge into the sea at Southwold, and Dunwich's once great naval importance vanished.

After Dunwich's eclipse as a port, the town itself then began to disappear into the sea as the soft cliff edge on which it was built gradually but steadily crumbled away beneath it. If you take the pretty cliff path that tunnels south through low woodland you can look out to sea over what was once the medieval town, and imagine whatever little may remain of its ruins of streets, houses and churches now stretching out invisibly for perhaps half a mile beneath the waves. Changing light and weather make this by turns an enchanting or an ominous view.

Now there is a single remaining church, a pleasant pub and, a few
houses along from it, a small but excellent museum about the
town's history (including the medieval Dunwich Seal (right). The
line of seaside houses is set unusually (but, given Dunwich's past,
sensibly) at right angles to the beach instead of perilously along
the cliff edge. The drawings opposite were made about ten years
ago. Now children play on the beach, parents bang the poles of
their windbreaks into the shingle, dogs swim in the waves, line-
fishermen sit under their umbrellas and families trudge along the
shingle with tea trays from the admirable wooden café where the
prospect of fish and chips and nautical banana splits for the
grandchildren is not far away.

Dunwich's overwhelming sight is the cliff. In summer, swarms of
sand martins fluttering frantically outside their holes in its sandy
cliff remind parents of the hectic business of bringing up families.
There are constant attempts to dissuade people from climbing up
the cliff and making it crumble still more. I've sometimes tried to
exaggerate its steepness by drawing from almost underneath it –
from further down the beach it looks less liable to topple over on
top of one. There is always a steady and inexorable tidal drift of
pebbles southward along this coast, and some ugly big black sackfuls
of stones have been half-sunk into the shingle in a Canute-like
attempt to stabilise it. You can walk a lonely mile or two south on
the beach beside the crumbling cliff until it disappears at Dunwich
Heath. On the way the cries of the waders and sea birds give the
place a wild intensity.

Although Dunwich's many original churches have long since tumbled off the cliff into the sea, you can still see the ruins of the priory of Grey Friars a bit further back from the edge – a classic sketchbook ruin with two tiers of stone arches but nothing behind them.

Down below at low tide the waves make intriguingly repetitive patterns in the shingle and sand, and there are wonderful unbroken perspectives along the beach. I've drawn and painted this scene many times, constantly intrigued here by the beauty and bleakness of sea, shingle and crumbling cliff under skies which are always changing with the light and the season. The pencil drawings were made quickly as studies, the watercolours opposite and overleaf took longer.

Further south along the shore, beyond Dunwich Heath and abreast of Minsmere, is a line of concrete wartime tank-traps called dragon's teeth; terns breed on the shingle between sea and sedge. At low tide all along this lonely beach the waves make repeat patterns in the shingle and sand, and there are unbroken perspectives along the beach – northwards towards Southwold's distant white lighthouse and south to Sizewell's nuclear power station. Its site must have been chosen for its lonely situation where a nuclear disaster would do minimum damage. I made the drawing above about thirty years ago; it includes the stark Sizewell A before it had been upstaged by the more alluring white concrete sphere of Sizewell B, which as a subject – rising moon or big ping-pong ball – I really prefer. Now you can drive right up to it and there is a visitor centre whose staff are at pains to explain how extremely safe everything is. From close to it nevertheless looks a bit awesome, but a few hundred yards to its south is a long beach, no less windy or shingly than any along this coast, with a café where we had lunch. Nearby were some fishing boats, one of them definitely still working. I drew it in the afternoon while Sue and the family lay on the shingle.

Aldeburgh's mixture of creative activity and the remains of a flourishing fishing industry is pervasive. Its wide shopping street is connected by narrow lanes to the seafront with its long line of hotels and low houses strung out like models beside the shifting shingle. The beach is rich in interesting objects: working fishing boats with their piratical-looking flags and buoys, and the rusty old caterpillar tractors that drag them up from the sea; their crates and plastic boxes and anchors, the shelving shingle itself, and its different stepped levels; the sea kale; the lifeboat and the two brick lookout towers; the down-to-earth vitality of the wooden fresh-fish-and-crab huts on the beach. The town is permeated by Aldeburgh's flourishing artistic and musical life, built on Britten, memorable in *Peter Grimes* performed on the beach (above) against the backdrop of real wooden fishing boats and the sea itself. It underpins and sustains the general vitality – coach loads of visitors, car parking in the churchyard, lectures in the Jubilee Hall, the thriving bookshop, the half-timbered cinema, the restaurants and pubs; the Moot Hall and the nearby ice-cream stall; Britten's and Pears' discreetly tucked-away Red House with its museum, library, archive and garden.

To either side of Aldeburgh stretch its magnificent shingle, tapering away south of the town to an alarmingly narrow strip between the sea and the yacht-filled Alde estuary. As one walks along it from the town, this strip seems to end with the picturesquely extravagant Martello tower tucked inside its horseshoe-shaped outer wall, but in reality the shingle then widens out again to continue much further as the wild and lonely Orford Ness, with its military debris. To the north the beach leads you past two metal monuments of our own time, a line of prosperously shimmering parked cars and Maggi Hambling's striking silvery steel *Scallop*, standing out defiantly against sea and sky. Seen from the side its asymmetrical silhouette reminded me of the Aldeburgh boat drawn thirty years ago, with its beautifully curving timbers. Further on you can see the jokey 1920s skyline of the holiday village of Thorpeness, and beyond this again the sober sphere of Sizewell.

The Suffolk coast is both enhanced and scarred by military relics. The stark medieval Orford Castle and the elegant Napoleonic Martello towers at Aldeburgh and Shingle Street were meant to defend people against attacks then thought imminent. So were the 1940s concrete roadside pill boxes and tank traps, rows of which remain half-sunk in the sand or shingle near high-water-mark at Bawdsey, Shingle Street and Dunwich, their purpose at least genuine and comprehensible. More sinister are the concrete pagodas on the wild shingle of Orford Ness, built around 1960 to try out detonators for nuclear bombs, their roofs raised on stilts over the test chambers ready to collapse and contain explosions that went wrong. When in 1993 the National Trust acquired most of the Ness, it left some of the military debris scattered about. In this bleakest of East Coast landscapes the pagodas stand as a macabre monument to the Cold War's dreary nuclear paranoia.

I first saw Shingle Street many years ago at dusk on an autumn evening when it seemed lonely, bleak and desolate. But when I was last there, on a windless June weekday, it seemed idyllic – a trim Martello tower and a row of nineteenth-century coastguard cottages, done-up but not spoiled. The shingle had its usual complex terraces and slopes with a gully just deep enough to conceal someone; there was a shingle islet just offshore but it's probably now drifted south. The pebbles didn't look particularly fertile but they sustained a spectacular crop of blue-green sea kale, growing in clumps up to about a metre across. There were comfortable-looking cars half-hidden among the marram grass and dunes, giving the place a slightly surreal yet middle-class air. Unlike the creepy relics of Orford Ness, Shingle Street looked peaceable and (in its better sense) human. Like Sizewell and Covehithe and many other places along the estuary-indented Suffolk coast it's at the end of the road – you can only get back the way you came. It seemed to embody this coast's character – its individuality, comfortable wildness and fragile beauty.

Much of the appeal of this coast, or indeed any coast, is that the sea is harder than the land to spoil. Besides neatly tidying up its shores with every tide, it appeals to the very idea of distance, mystery and the unknown. Things are naturally different inland, where the marks of man's hand on the countryside, whether for better or worse, are inescapable wherever one looks. The appeal of the pleasingly undramatic and even slightly backward part of the countryside seen in this book is that our century's confident aspirations for growth and wealth creation at any price have not yet taken overall charge here; the raw materials of the main industry, farming, are things we instinctively value and respect – land, space, nature, greenery and crops. These make up the landscapes, views and details that have long been thought worth cherishing, and which have the added appeal of being not merely desirable but real.

List of pictures

Most of the drawings and
watercolours in this book were
made between 1979 when we
first came to Huntingfield and
2014. The exceptions are the
watercolours of Ipswich Dock,
1955 and Woodbridge Tide
Mill, 1966, made when it was
still clad in corrugated iron.

First published in 2014 by Full Circle Editions

Text copyright © David Gentleman 2014

Paintings and drawings copyright © David Gentleman 2014

The moral right of the author has been asserted

Design and Layout copyright © Full Circle Editions 2014
Parham House Barn, Brick Lane, Framlingham, Woodbridge, Suffolk IP13 9LQ
www.fullcircle–editions.co.uk

Set in New Baskerville & Gill Sans
Paper: Munken Pure 120gsm from FSC® Mix Credit

Book design: David Gentleman and Jonathan Christie

Thanks to Dean Hearn at Healeys for his work on the picture scans

Printed and bound in Suffolk by Healeys Print Group, Ipswich

ISBN 978-0-9571528-5-4

Note on the typeface:
Baskerville is a transitional serif typeface designed in 1757 by John Baskerville (1706–75) and was an attempt to improve upon the types of William Caslon. Baskerville increased the contrast between thick and thin strokes, making the serifs sharper and more tapered, and shifted the axis of rounded letters to a more vertical position. The curved strokes are more circular in shape, and the characters became more regular. These changes created a greater consistency in size and form, although the perfection of his work seems to have unsettled his contemporaries, and some claimed the stark contrasts in his printing damaged the eyes. Abroad, however, he was much admired, notably by Fournier & Bodoni. *Baskerville* was revived in 1917 by Bruce Rogers for the Harvard University Press and in 1923 in England by Stanley Morison for the British Monotype Company. *New Baskerville* was designed by Matthew Carter and John Quaranda in 1978.